From Photoshop to Dreamweaver

3 Steps to Great Visual Web Design

Credits

Authors
Colin Smith
Crystal Waters

Commissioning Editor
Luke Harvey

Graphic Editor
Avtar Bhogal

Editors
Alan McCann
Paul Thewlis

Cover Design
Katy Freer
Avtar Bhogal

Indexer
Simon Collins

Author Agent
Chris Matterface

Project Manager
Simon Brand

Technical Reviewers
Martin White
Jon Steer
Kim Christensen
Clifton Evans
Tim Payne
Vicki Loader
Dan Caylor
Chris Arlidge
Matthew B. Hein

Proof Reader
Mel Orgee

Managing Editor
Chris Hindley

AUTHOR BIOGRAPHIES

Colin Smith   www.photoshopCAFE.com

Colin is an award winning Graphic Designer who has caused a stir in the design community with his stunning photorealistic illustrations composed entirely in Photoshop. He is also founder of the popular PhotoshopCafe web resource for Photoshop users and web designers. He has won numerous design contests and awards, including Guru Awards at the 2001 Photoshop World Convention in LA, 2002 in SanDiego and MacWorld 2002 in NY. Colin's work has been recognized by Photoshop User, Mac Design, Dynamic Graphics, Computer Arts, Studio Multimedia and WWW Internet Life magazines. Colin is also a regular columnist for the NAPP members' site and Planet Photoshop. Between Freelance Design and writing for foED, he keeps pretty busy. Colin has co authored New Masters of Photoshop, Foundation Photoshop, Photoshop Most Wanted and Photoshop 7 Trade Secrets.

"To Jason Cook, my Dreamweaver teacher, thanks for all the extra help on UltraDev."

Crystal Waters

Crystal has been writing about consumer-oriented technology since the '80s – back when 5MB hard drives were a novel upgrade! She's author of two books, *Web Concept & Design* and *Universal Web Design* (New Riders), and also co-author of *The Flash Usability Guide* from foED. She's been an editor at a number of magazines and was director of MFWeb conferences, among other roles. Crystal is a long-distance charity cyclist and avid kayak-fisherman. She lives and fishes with her boyfriend Dwayne (who took this photo) and dog Nellie (pictured) in Vermont. Her sites are www.typo.com and www.girlbike.com. She likes parentheses (obviously) – and, erm, dashes.

From Photoshop to Dreamweaver

Dreamweaver

3 Steps to Great Visual Web Design

Colin Smith
Crystal Waters

From Photoshop to Dreamweaver

3 Steps to Great Visual Web Design

© 2002 friends of ED

First Printed November 2002

Trademark Acknowledgements

friends of ED has endeavored to provide trademark information about all the companies and products mentioned in this book by the appropriate use of capitals. However, friends of ED cannot guarantee the accuracy of this information.

Published by friends of ED

30-32 Lincoln Road, Olton, Birmingham.
B27 6PA. UK.
Printed in USA

ISBN 1-903450-57-8

6 More advanced web techniques   181

7 Getting your site online   217

Photoshop and Dreamweaver Pro Tips   235

Welcome

Welcome to *From Photoshop To Dreamweaver*. In just 250 pages time, you'll be effortlessly designing websites using the two best design tools out there, and you'll be effectively and efficiently planning, optimizing and publishing websites before you know it.

You'll want to get started as soon as possible so we don't intend to keep you waiting; there's just a few quick things you should know before you get going.

The Book Format

The book is sorted into three sections, reflecting our easy three-step process:

Plan and Design

Plan and Design – Here we'll be mainly using Photoshop to conjure the visuals of our site, drafting some layouts and designing buttons, and tabs, before adding in images and placeholders for text.

Create and Streamline

Create and Streamline – Using ImageReady, we'll be optimizing our site for the Web and looking at some different ways to add interactivity. Then, in Dreamweaver, we'll show you how to streamline your processes and save a lot of time.

Enhance and Publish

Enhance and Publish – Still mainly in Dreamweaver in this last section, we'll add some advanced effects as well as some animation in ImageReady, before taking you step-by-step through the process of getting your website online. We finish off with nearly 20 top professional tips for getting the most from your new skills.

We don't use very many styles throughout the book, but we do emphasize special tips of particularly important points like this:

> *This is a tip; remember me, and maybe even pass me onto your friends!*

Support and Feedback

All books from friends of ED aim to be easy to follow and without errors. However, if you do run into problems, don't hesitate to e-mail us – our support is **fast**, **friendly**, and **free**.

You can reach us at support@friendsofED.com, quoting the last four digits of the ISBN in the subject of the e-mail (that's 0578 in this case). If you're having technical problems with a specific file that you've created from an exercise, it can sometimes help to include a copy of that file with your mail.

Even if our dedicated reader support team is unable to solve your problem immediately, your queries will be passed onto the people who put the book together – the editors and authors – to solve.

Technical queries aside, we'd love to hear from you, whether it's to request future books, ask about friends of ED, or tell us about the sites you went on to create after reading *From Photoshop to Dreamweaver*.

> *To tell us a bit about yourself and make comments about the book, why not fill out the reply card at the back and send it to us!*

Friends of ED also run a wide range of design community forums at www.friendsofed.com/forums. Head along there for some information, inspiration or just plain chat, and don't forget to keep visiting www.friendsofed.com for news, more books, sample chapters, downloads, author interviews and more!

OK, that's enough info to get you started. Turn the page and we'll start our journey around the world of possibilities Photoshop, ImageReady and Dreamweaver have to offer.

1 Planning your website

In this chapter...

We introduce the Photoshop and Dreamweaver partnership and discuss why we have chosen to use this pairing for the book, moving on then to think about planning our design for the Web, covering:

- Print vs web – designing for the Internet
- Planning your website and brainstorming ideas
- Thinking about your site content and wireframing
- Design principles and color theory
- Customizing your color palette in Photoshop
- Organizing your site's navigation

Why Photoshop and Dreamweaver?

We chose these two applications, Adobe Photoshop and Macromedia Dreamweaver, because they are arguably the most popular programs out there that people use together for web design, and agree there is good reason for it. These programs are from competing companies – both publish software for manipulating images, and both publish website layout applications. While some people may prefer to have all applications from the same publisher to assure file compatibility or to stay loyal to a favorite vendor, the fact remains that most people use Photoshop for images, and Dreamweaver for web page layout.

We will be using Photoshop, ImageReady and Dreamweaver extensively throughout this book. We'll be teaching ImageReady and Dreamweaver techniques from the ground up, but will expect that you have some Photoshop knowledge already, even if you have only previously used it for print or graphic design.

Introducing Dreamweaver MX

Dreamweaver was born in December 1997, to applause and accolades for its first attempt at successful integration of web layout and HTML hand-coding. It didn't add unnecessary code, or change what you were trying to do. It also let you add your own code if you wanted to. It gave a pretty good approximation of what your site would really look like in a browser, and allowed designers to do some funky stuff if they wanted to. Lo and behold, it had easy table-making facilities, site management tools, and built-in support for various formatting standards.

But best of all, it gave designers the ability to make sites look like what they had in their minds, within the limitations of the web browsers and systems of the day. A bonus was that it was relatively easy to learn and use, although its depth of features can take time and lots of practice to master.

Dreamweaver took over, almost from the start, as the preferred tool for web page layout and site management by most professional web designers. It also has a good community of users and developers who write behaviors and extensions (add-ins that append enhanced features for increased functionality) for the program. Macromedia forums are a particularly good resource for ideas, tips, and assistance.

> *Macromedia offer a free 30-day trial of the latest version of Dreamweaver MX. If you're not sure about laying out a chunk of cash until you give the program a serious try, downloading this fully functional trial is a good way to give Dreamweaver a test run, especially with what you'll learn in this book*

Dreamweaver MX can seem a bit overwhelming when some of its features are uncovered, but the 'power-to-ease quotient' is actually quite appealing.

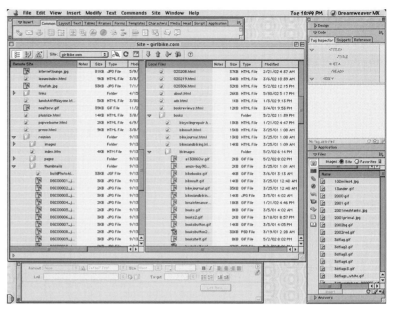

The key appeal of Dreamweaver has always been its WYSIWYG abilities. Here you see it in Dreamweaver MX...

...and here it is in my browser, exactly as I had intended it to look.

For those not design-inclined, Dreamweaver MX includes a number of templates to get a lot of people started with good, basic, functional designs.

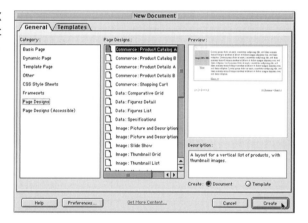

You still have a lot of work to do before and after you pick a design, from determining the goal of the site, to how to best reach your audience, what your site will include for content, color schemes, and so on. We'll cover these throughout this opening chapter.

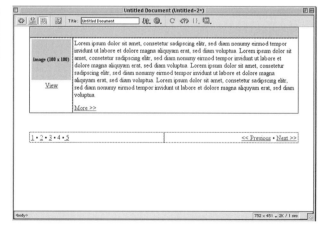

Print vs. web: Photoshop experience transformed

If you've had experience with Photoshop, but not with the Web, you've probably been designing for print. This could be individual images for portfolio or decorative purposes, manipulating photos for family photo albums, or image manipulation for catalogs, newsletters, magazines, flyers, or other print media.

While working in Photoshop, you probably learned very quickly that a beautiful feature of it, like any software, is that you can change anything at any time to suit your visual desires. Once a piece is printed, such as a newsletter or magazine, it's a lot tougher to make changes unless you go through every copy with a permanent marker. In other words, it's not something you really want to spend your afternoon doing.

The beauty of web publishing, of course, is that no matter what you publish, you can change nearly anything at any time.

This beauty of flexibility and creative opportunities, however, has its dark side. If you were around during the early days of desktop publishing, you may remember the dreaded 'ransom note' designs that found their way into newsletters and other self-published documents. Novice designers had access to every font family and every way of presenting type *and* photos *and* clip art *and* borders *and* drop-shadows. Used with finesse, any of these elements can make a design stand out. Used with excessive enthusiasm, bunching a number of these elements together makes for horrid design possibilities. Unfortunately, a number of websites still feature this scary combination of features.

Designers may also remember when clients found out that their publications could be changed all the way up until a piece was at the printer – they would call at the eleventh hour demanding an image swap, editorial changes, or even total redesign. While it could be done, it wasn't the ideal way for the project to go smoothly.

The web gave us the ability to change content of a 'finished' document whenever we wished. All documents are dynamic in the sense that the web designer can overwrite information, reorganize the structure, add or delete images and page elements, change color schemes - anything, you name it - at any given moment.

Images for the Web

The Web uses two main types of image for their compression and cross-platform accessibility. A third is also supported by an increasing number of browsers.

Probably the most popular format is the **GIF** (Graphics Interchange Format, pronounced with either a hard or soft 'g'). This is a type of image compression for bitmapped images. It has been used for years, long before the web came about. Its compression scheme works ideally on images with flat colors, rather than photographs or images with a lot of dithering. They can also be animated, and support transparency, which is one of the reasons they are so widely used. They are also ideal for buttons and icons – anything with no need for lots of colors.

JPEGs (an acronym of Joint Photographic Experts Group, pronounced 'jay-peg') are generally best used on images with lots of subtle changes in colors, such as photographs. The format's compression method is lossy, meaning that it cuts out (or loses) colors and approximates them with colors within the new limited palette. The lower the quality, the fewer the colors to choose from, and quality gets worse. The benefit of using JPEG files is that you can save them as 24-bit images (16 million colors), so if they are decompressed on someone's screen that happens to have a monitor set to that resolution, they can appreciate the higher quality.

This Save for Web comparison in Photoshop shows the above text/flat color file with a few different options. Note that the bottom two images are how it would look saved as a JPEG. Even the high-quality JPEG ends up with artifacts – the wiggly stuff around the edges of the letter. The image on the top right is a GIF.

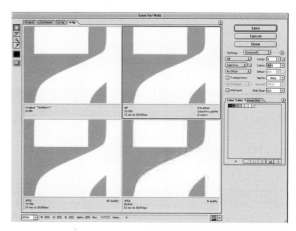

In contrast, a photograph is best saved as a JPEG. The upper right image is a high quality JPEG option, while the two bottom images represent what the photo would look like as a GIF, even if saved at highest quality (left, bottom).

PNG (Portable Network Graphics, pronounced 'ping') is a graphics format born of concern that we'd all have to pay licensing fees to use GIF images on our websites. It was designed from the beginning to replace GIFs, and created smaller files with better quality than GIFs. The most impressive features of PNG graphics is that they support alpha transparency, which allows you to include effects like drop-shadows and anti-aliasing against any background, unlike its graphic counterparts.

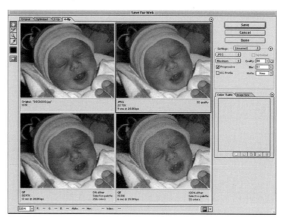

While PNG is supported by nearly every browser out there, Microsoft Internet Explorer for Windows, the most popular of browsers, still doesn't support its alpha channel features, so PNG isn't a high priority with web designers. Ironically, the Macintosh version of Internet Explorer gets the highest rating for most supportive of the PNG format, but that's not enough for designers to exchange all their GIFs and JPEGs for PNGs quite yet.

Planning your website

If you've figured out at least to some degree what you want to put on your site, then the next step (and you've probably thought about this long before deciding content or layout) is to determine some of the aesthetic values of your site. What a site looks like, and the impression it makes, is crucial to its success, and one of the first elements of the planning process. A fundamental element that stands out in putting together site aesthetics is exploring color and color schemes, and we'll do this later, but first you need to thoroughly plan out what you intend your site to do.

What is the goal of your site?

Just who are you making this site for, and what do you hope to accomplish with it? In the process of preparing to create or redesign a site, one of the first things you have to determine is your objective for the site. If your goal is simply to make a site for practice reasons while you're reading through this book, that's fine. Reasons you might want to make a site can be serious or trivial, complicated or simple. Perhaps you want to grow your business, showcase a portfolio, market a local non-profit organization, make money, sell a product, impress people, find clients, or simply to have another outlet for your work or words. It doesn't matter what your goal is, but you do have to get a fairly firm grip on what it is.

Some of the questions to ask yourself to help you narrow down your site's goal include:

- Do I hope to make money with the site?

- Do I want to sell my services with it, or find a job with it?

- Do I want to make a site to act as a family photo album or diary?

- Is it to advertise my already-existing business?

- Is it to sell my product?

- Is it to raise awareness of a topic?

It's fine to have more than one goal (to raise awareness about pollution, and to sell your services as a health consultant, for example). With the goal in mind, you'll then go on to determine what the site is about.

What is your site about?

Now that you know your goal, what is your site about? For example, if your goal is to sell a product, what is your product? If you were an importer of Icelandic sweaters, your site would probably be a catalog format. Perhaps you want to include information about Icelandic wool, a gallery of custom knit work, price lists, and so on. Start with a brainstorming list, and categorize the items you come up with.

Brainstorming is an ideal way to get a feel for all of the kinds of topics and elements you want to include in your site, before you come close to even thinking about how the information will be organized. Brainstorming is literally writing down every single idea you might have about a site without judgement or analysis, no matter how silly, or trivial, or all-consuming it may seem. Later on, you'll worry about organizing, cutting, categorizing, and so on.

It should continue as long as you come up with ideas. Some of the topics may seem irrelevant, but if they come to mind, write them down. No one needs to see this but you, or your planning team.

How would you evaluate your audience?

So who are these folks who will be coming to your site? Do you know their age range, spending power, or color preferences? Who needs your site, and who wants it? How will they find out about it? These kinds of demographics and facts about your audience, gathered formally or informally, will help you determine everything from color schemes, type sizes, tone of voice, and overall design. Depending on who they are, they might like something brightly colored and youth-oriented, or sophisticated and refined.

You can come up with an idea of who your site is for by creating another list to refer to during your planning. Let's say you're creating a site with the goal to promote your illustration skills. You want to get freelance jobs, both short and long-term contracts. Who do you want to come see your site?

- Art directors who hire freelance illustrators

- Magazine editors

- Publishers

- Advertising firms

- Web designers

- Companies with big budgets who will pay you lots of money, on time

- People who have fast connections to the web that can view your high-res images

In your case, perhaps the sex and age (among other factors) of your site visitors is irrelevant, since that doesn't determine if you are hired as an illustrator. Location of the user (since they may want you to work in-house), job level (you want someone who can actually hire you or influence your hiring), and type of company (a company with the need for illustrators), for example, would be relevant features of your target audience.

How do you want to impress your audience?

How do you want your website to come across? Do you want your site to impress your audience with its complicated navigation, or want to get your audience to go to as many pages as possible without necessarily using the latest software tricks? One doesn't necessarily rule out the other, but your goals should help you prioritize how you'll want to present your site. If your goal is to sell your services as a designer to game developers, then an elaborate presentation with accompanying boom-box music would be much more appropriate than if you're selling Victorian wallpaper and window treatments.

What is your strategy?

Do you have a strategy plan for your site? Who are your competitors, and how do you see yourself standing up against them? Answers to these questions can also determine color schemes, content, and design. For example, if you're creating a website for a local bookstore, you're not only going up against other local bookstores, but all the big guys such as Amazon and Barnes & Noble. Everything's a level playing field on the Web.

Your color scheme would probably be strongly suggestive of your logo colors, and therefore recognizable to your audience, if they are repeat customers. The content you provide would probably best be targeted toward providing local information, such as book signings and readings at your store, as well as local events that your store might sponsor or otherwise be involved in.

The design would be determined by a number of factors. If you only sold comic books, perhaps it would have a 'comic' feel, with primary colors and popular action figures and illustrated novel characters featured. If you concentrate on children's books, primary colors and downloadable children's activities may be an idea, whereas if you sell how-to household books, your site may include excerpts from popular how-to-do-your-own-plumbing books or areas of the site might be fashioned after popular interior decorating themes of the time.

Do you intend to sell or market a product?

If you're planning to sell things, this determines site structure, navigation, and other design elements. Selling products also greatly affects the initial hiring of an appropriate web-hosting service that has experience with helping people set up and support storefronts to help clients have a safe transaction, and process orders correctly. Talk with your local service provider and see how they might help you. Ask for URLs of other sites they have helped to develop, and currently host, to see if their shopping carts and processing features are those that would work for you.

Site and content development

Once you've taken care of the first part of the website planning process – defining what you want to do with your site, determining its goals, looking at your potential audience, and the strategies for getting them to stay in your site and come back again – the next part of site design is planning the site's structure. Organization is crucial for site success, because if someone can't get to what they want, then there's no reason to have it there in the first place. No matter what kind of site you decide to build, no matter what kind of design you end up with, consistent, logical structure is necessary groundwork for the entire project, both in initial design and in later updates. Each page, each piece of content, the overall site, the visual design, and the overall experience for each page depend on it.

Developing site structure is also crucial for your own use. Whether it's for initial site organization and launch, or for updates down the road, determining a consistent design and structure for each page, the site, and the content only serves to streamline the entire process.

The information you're presenting needs to be organized in order to be comprehended and navigable by the reader or end-user. Imagine this book without a table of contents, without chapter separations, no page numbers, without an index, and no paragraph headings, just text text text text text. Even fictional books, which tend to not have subheadings and indexes, generally have chapters in which the action changes view, or we move to another character or timeframe. The only hint we have of what 'direction' to take in such a case is that we know by years of habit and training that we start at one of a book and can go through to the other end.

Brainstorming

My first suggestion to people when they're planning to fill up a site is to first just start brainstorming anything and everything that is relevant to the site's content. At this stage, there's no reason to be worried about structure or organization – it's a lot easier to structure a site if you have a list of topics to organize.

The easiest way for me to do this is simply with a pad of paper and a pencil, or a chalkboard or whiteboard, if those are available. The bigger wall-mounted media is best if you're working with a group, so everyone can see all of the ideas all of the time. Another option is to start out with a huge pile of index cards or 3" x 5" self-stick notes, and write each thing you brainstorm on each card or note. I tend to start out with a list and then transcribe each item over to a note or card; either way is fine. Whatever's easier for your brain to storm to.

Now just start writing. Don't think about order or reason or logic at this point, just write down every idea you have, no matter how trivial you think it might be.

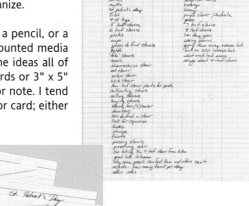

Next step, unless I start with cards instead of a list, is to transfer each topic to an index card or sticky-note.

Now's the time to work on deciding on top-level content categories. Pick up your pile of index cards or sticky notes, and start laying them out, like you're dealing a deck of cards. Those that seem similar should go in the same pile. After a while, you should see a pattern emerge.

As I start to lay out my cards for my site, I find that some categories are similar. Then other categories start to relate to the main categories.

I've rearranged my cards and also used outline sketches to work on finding the top-level content areas of my site. Here's one version of a sketch with some of the original ideas for content. I ended up with a few versions before I landed the one chosen.

Once you've brainstormed some headings and subject areas, these can form into a rough list of your website's sections and pages. Next you need to decide what form those pages are going to take.

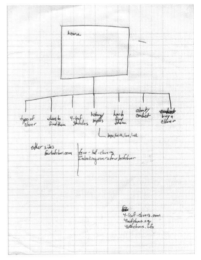

Wireframing

Wireframing is a term used to describe blocking out a page design into the parts that will eventually be filled with content. For example, a simple wireframe for a basic site might be:

Most sites contain a lot more elements than this, such as advertisements, search forms, a secondary navigational menu, feature stories or company news flashes, a sign-in area, and so on.

A simple wireframed page layout.

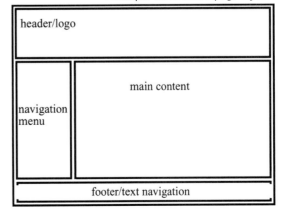

As you start to create wireframes for your site, you'll be using them as visual reminders for page layout, to remind you to include elements on appropriate pages, and to keep naming conventions on your site consistent. Sites often contain more than one wireframe convention; many sites have a splash page for the home page (like the cover of a magazine), then a content layout wireframe within the site (like magazine pages), and various other wireframe layouts, depending on the content.

Design principles

As both developer and browser software get more advanced, computers get faster and more powerful, and more people access the Web every day, the variables of a successful site change. It can be overwhelming to keep on top of software and market developments, even for those entrenched in the industry.

Luckily, there are basic, common principles of web design that always stay true in the formula for a good site ... or at least, almost always. And while we won't even begin to pretend that this chapter will be able to convey everything you've ever wanted to know about basic web design, we'll let you in on some of the most basic principles, challenges, and tips to get started. As you go through the book, you'll see these in action.

> *If you have done print design, you may have an advantage over those new to design. It won't make web design suddenly easy, but still, many of the design principles you've learned in creating page layouts remain true to the Web.*

Using color as a messenger

Color is used in our everyday lives to describe suggest all kinds of things, from states of mind to awkward situations. We say we're 'feeling blue' or 'green with envy'. We get 'caught red handed' telling 'little white lies', and are 'yellow' if we don't own up to it. Color plays an integral part in explaining how a person feels and how they act, and helps to display a person's personality or features.

Societies all over the world have established color rules or traditions for various events and meanings, such as the Western standards of white for a wedding dress. In India, however, bride's wedding dresses are often pink and red saris, a Turkish bride might wear a bright red cape over her dress, and an Armenian bride may wear a red silk wedding gown. Most funeral etiquette requests that attendees wear black or dark colors, but a sample exception is that at traditional Chinese funerals the men wear dark colors and women wear white.

As times change, different colors and color patterns become acceptable: read any fashion magazine to see a dozen examples. In short, color generally means more than what meets the eye. You needn't be an expert in color theory or therapy, but if you are targeting a particular product or service to a country or region, your color scheme should mean what you intend it to mean.

In Western culture, colors have a number of common associations, like *black* connoting night, mourning, or evil, *white* suggesting innocence or authority (e.g. doctor's coats), or *red* meaning anything from love and romance, to fire and anger.

Color theory and harmony have been fields of study for quite a long time by artists and psychologists alike, and a quick search on the web will find you more resources than you'll ever want. There are fascinating concepts of how colors affect mood, purchasing decisions, and many other feelings and actions. Have you noticed, for example, that the majority of food product labels have red as a main color? That kids' toy packages are yellow with other primary colors? That the packaging of feminine care products is in pastels with soft edged images and cursive lettering, while fishing gear products, generally marketed to males, are often marketed with dark colors with bright holographic chrome lettering?

Contrasting for readability

A crucial consideration for choosing a smart color scheme is making sure that there is contrast between the text or other elements, and the background of the pages. The default color scheme for most browsers is a gray background with black text, blue links, and purple visited links. That color scheme, although maybe a little boring, happens to be a good one for reading comfortably.

There are many guidelines about on-screen readability, such as using a dark text on a light background, but the easiest measurement of readability and sufficient element contrast is to just see if you can read it yourself. If you can't read it or discern among objects on the screen, your audience probably can't either.

The easier it is for you to read something, the easier it is for others. The more the color values are similar, the least amount of contrast for the overall image. The best bet is opposing values, whether using the same hue or not, and so for our purposes the one in the middle is the best.

While different platforms and different monitor settings will make colors appear differently, viewing a site on nearly any monitor with any graphic browser will give you enough of an approximation of at least the readability of the information on a page. PC monitors tend to show colors darker than Mac monitors, but if two colors contrast strongly on the Mac, they should still contrast strongly on a PC.

If you're still not sure whether a color scheme offers enough contrast, switch your monitor to show grayscale only. If items fall out of the picture, or you're unable to see them anymore, those items need a value change. Keep testing this until it's easy to discern among elements.

These are things you might want to keep in mind now as we move on to defining the colors for our site.

Web color defaults

If you've been using Photoshop for primarily print publications, chances are your color settings are set for print defaults or customized to your print specifications. While most people have graduated to monitors that support more than 256 colors, if you're not sure of your market, it may be better to play it safe. If your market includes non-profit companies, or schools with low budgets that might not be able to upgrade systems as fast as a well-endowed company, Photoshop's web graphics defaults will best suit the most systems. Its web color settings will be more than adequate for most of your web image production needs, and optimize settings to best create images for viewing on the web.

- To check whether Photoshop is set to web color defaults, and to change it if it's not, first choose Color Setting from the Edit menu.

- If your settings aren't already set to Web Graphics Defaults, choose that setting from the pop-up Settings menu.

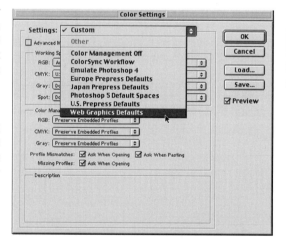

Why is this important? Mostly because the web is still viewed by multiple millions of people on multiple millions of variations of computer systems, and these settings best set up image brightness and quality for as many monitors and web standards as possible. Of course, you can always change settings down the road as you see fit. For example, if you do a survey and find out that most of your target market views the web from Mac monitors rather than PC monitors, you will want to design with Mac monitor gamma in mind. The Web Graphics Default settings are set up for PC monitors, since they represent the majority of systems for the overall web-viewing market.

Picking a color palette

You might be starting to think of the color scheme for your site, or perhaps you have a logo or image on which you'll be basing color choices. Your color palette may be limited by a client decision, or it may be limited or extended to include company logo colors, a state or country flag colors, organizational uniform colors, holiday-specific color schemes, and so on.

If you've got to keep your client's or company's artwork and site within a specific color palette, you can customize a swatch just for your own use, or for each project, if you want. It can be tedious work, but if your design has to be very specific this can save time in the long run on a big project. Some companies get very fussy about keeping their logo colors intact and color themes unblemished, and some also follow very stringent accessibility guidelines to assist those with color blindness and other visual impairments.

Customizing your palette

1.   Pick a swatch to start from, by choosing from the drop-down menu. I've chosen the Web Hues swatch palette.

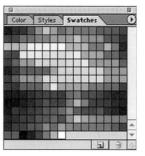

2.   Find a color you don't want in your palette anymore. If you click and hold down your mouse button on a swatch, a little grabber hand appears. You can now drag that color to the trash.

> *You may also hold down* CTRL+ALT *(or* OPTION+APPLE*) keys, and click on the color you wish to remove when the scissors appear.*

3. Keep on dragging colors to the trash until you get down to the palette you want.

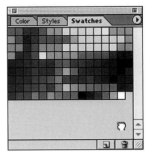

4. If you need to add colors from your logo or another image, open it and use the eyedropper to select the color you want (it becomes the foreground color).

5. Click on the Create New Swatch icon at the bottom of the swatches palette and the foreground color will be added. You can also move your cursor over the gray part of the palette. A paint bucket appears and you can then just click to add the color to the swatch display.

Your custom color is now on your palette.

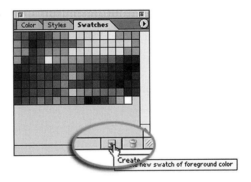

6. Choose Save Swatches from the menu.

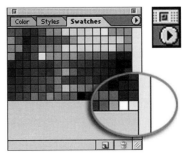

7. If you want your new swatch to appear on your drop-down menu, make sure you save it in the Color Swatches folder, found in Photoshop > Presets.

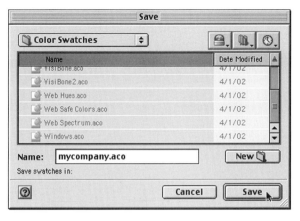

8. The next time you open Photoshop, your custom swatch will be listed on the Swatches panel menu.

Successful color scheme samples

There are more elements to a successful website than its color scheme, but a tour around the web looking at various markets shows that there are certain colors that seem to be present within the same kinds of sites, or a range of values for similar sites within a market. For example, while I couldn't make the claim that dark blue is the color of choice of all newspapers, an informal survey of newspaper sites shows that a great many papers chose dark blue as a main color for either headlines or navigational buttons and backgrounds.

Consider our color discussions early on in this chapter, and think about what dark blue is often associated with. Dark blue is a common association for business, and at various times in the fashion cycle, is a choice color for business suits. It's a serious color without being somber. Imagine if a newspaper site was bright orange and neon green – we'd be less likely to take the news seriously, wouldn't we?

All around the US, newspapers often use dark blue as a base color for their sites. Main content areas, though, are white with dark text, for high contrast readability. From left to right: www.washingtonpost.com, www.statesman.com, www.burlingtonfreepress.com, www.signonsandiego.com, www.adn.com, and www.suntimes.com.

Internationally, newspapers may take on other color schemes, but most are still very 'serious' in their color choices. From Rio de Janeiro, Brazil (http://jbonline.terra.com.br), London (www.timesonline.co.uk), New Delhi, India (http://timesofindia.indiatimes.com), New Zealand (www.nzherald.co.nz), Kenya, Africa (www.nationaudio.com) to Bangkok, Thailand (www.bangkokpost.net), newspapers attempt to give serious news a serious look.

Similarly, and maybe obviously, no matter what the chocolate, brown is the anchor color of choice. Here are www.godiva.com, www.ghirardelli.com, www.lakechamplain chocolate.com, and http://herseys.com as examples.

From a walk through a grocery store to a browse on the web, it's obvious that color has both strong and subtle impacts on our mood and our attention, and conveys varying messages depending on the conforms of the culture we happen to be in. Colors are associated with sexes, ages, organizations, brands, and affiliations. Barbie boxes are pink, red carpets lead us to galas. Color can tell people what we are about even before they read a word on our pages.

We don't have room here to include an exhaustive reference list of how each color fits each market, or how each color is accepted (or rejected) in various countries and cultures, by various age groups or other target markets. It's apparent, however, that color does make a site's first impression much more effective, and it's worth the research to figure out what scheme will work best for your market.

Now that we're armed with color theories and practices, schemes and examples, it's time to move on to web navigational theory so we can start putting projects together, and getting people where we want them to go in our sites.

There are few things more important to a site's success than its navigational scheme, hand in hand with site organization. The basic rule of thumb at play here is that if someone is comfortable getting around your site, then they will probably spend more time there, and enjoy the experience, and probably even return in the future, perhaps multiple times. No matter how gorgeous your graphics, innovative your design, or snappy your color scheme, if it doesn't help people get around your site and find what they want, it might as well not even be there.

But before you even think about how to get people to areas on your site, you'll have to do some site planning. Brainstorming content ideas, looking at various ways of organizing information, doing draft layouts, playing with navigational schemes, all of these work together.

Navigation necessities

The best tip for making your site navigationally sound is that you should use what works. By no means does this mean that you have to make your site look like everyone else's, but it's best to follow a few simple suggestions that help to assure that your navigational scheme will work.

Use understandable icons

Not every site designer is going to use icons for site navigation, but if you do, be sure to make sure that they make sense. For example, icons that have become standard on the web are the shopping cart for shopping, and an envelope for sending email. A magnifying glass is often used for a search icon.

If you decide to use your own icons that perhaps others may not recognize, then be sure to label your icons, if not on every page, then at the top level and in an easily accessed help area. You can also use ALT text to enable a pop-up tooltip when users roll their mouse over your link.

Use breadcrumbs

If you remember your Hansel and Gretel fairy tale, breadcrumbs are what they left so that they would find their way back home when they were taken into the wood to be left to die. While the breadcrumbs didn't work out so well in the book, on the web, they serve as a guideline back to where you started, as well as a reminder of where in the hierarchy you are at the moment

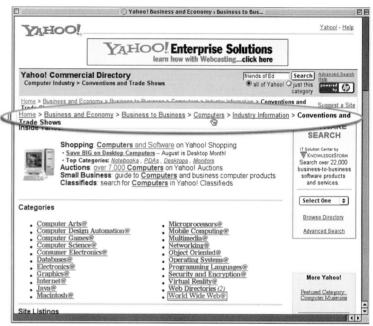

Yahoo! has used breadcrumbs since its inception. Whether you followed this path to a particular category listing or not, Yahoo gives the most direct path back to the top. The angle bracket is a common breadcrumb signifier.

Don't hide information

Unless you're creating a site that includes interactive hide-and-seek, don't hide information either by making links inconspicuous, or by putting information down tenlayers of clicks. If someone has to click more than a couple of times to get to information they want, then there is probably a navigational structure problem.

Help people out

You don't generally need to explain and label everything everywhere on a site, and unless your users are web neophytes coming to your site to learn how to navigate the Web, then you don't need to provide lessons on how to use a website. But you should include easily accessible information that explains anything that is exclusive to your site, whether it be as simple as contact information for those who have questions about finding information, downloading and software installation instructions if that's applicable, or instructions on how to fill out a specific form.

A site map, like a book's table of contents, or an on-screen guide for television shows, is an easy way to give people guidance and an idea of your content structure. A well-organized site map is a good place for people to find things quickly and navigate from deeper levels than top level navigation. If your site has hundreds of pages, then you won't want to include the title of every page, but you will want to include perhaps three levels of information. Like a book, you wouldn't want to have a table of contents that listed every paragraph, but you would want every chapter and perhaps a subheading to help you find information more readily.

Summary

Organization, navigation, layout and color scheme needn't be the same for every site that exists, but by following a few simple guidelines, users (including you) will be more apt to be able to find what they want, go where they want to go, and know where they are at all times. Navigation isn't about being the same, it's just about being consistent and clear.

Now we'll start doing more hands-on site building throughout the next few chapters, using the tools and techniques in this last chapter and pulling together a working project.

We'll begin by constructing a more solid site mock-up from which to build the working site which will form our case study for the rest of the book. This will allow us to put everything we've learned here into practice; we can then move into Dreamweaver and start creating a real website from scratch.

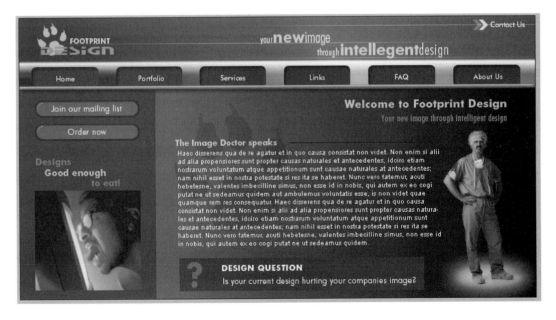

2 Designing our site in Photoshop

In this chapter...

We take our site ideas, our planning and design decisions, and put them into action, building a Photoshop mock-up of our site site that includes:

- The navigation bar
- Some visual effects
- A logo we'll design from scratch
- Some dummy text to act as a placeholder
- Some dummy images

We've looked at some of the basics and principles of the web. We've covered planning out our site and storyboarding it on paper. Now it's time to get our feet wet and start focusing on the steps we'll take to create a real working website.

A very common practice in web design is to create a mock-up in Photoshop. The mock-up is a visual representation of the finished design. The purpose of the mock-up is to get client approval on the look and feel of the website without spending any unnecessary time on HTML and features. It's usually quicker and easier to move things around and experiment with Photoshop than it would be on an actual web page.

The mock-up will be non-functioning, but it won't be wasted time. When the mock-up is approved by the client, or boss (depending on whether you're freelance or work for a company), it will then be easy to slice the image and turn it into a working website. This is the way many professionals approach web design and it's exactly what you're going to learn in this book. You'll be following the path that professionals take and learning good habits right off the bat.

> For this purpose we'll be concentrating on Photoshop in this chapter; Dreamweaver will come into play in **Chapter 4**.

I just want to make it clear at this point that you should be creative and create an original site. The examples in this book are for demonstration purposes only and not intended to say, "This is the right way", or, "This is the only way to lay out your web page". You can follow along with the example project if you wish, or adapt the techniques for your own creation. There are obviously things that will work better than others, but the only right way is the way that will work best for your particular needs. You'll learn techniques that you can adapt and apply to various projects, and a workflow that you can apply to all your projects. We're teaching you a framework only and you will need to adapt it for your personal preferences.

So without further rambling by me, let's get into it!

The first thing we need to do it determine the size of your web page. There are many factors to take into consideration. The main one is screen resolution.

People will be using resolutions as diverse as 640x480 pixels to 1600x1024 and even beyond. Obviously your website will look very different on each configuration. A practice that used to be very popular was to set the page size to stretch and fit any resolution, using repeating patterns for the background. The advantage of this method is that no matter what size screen is being used, the page will expand to fit the entire screen. The disadvantage is that the designer has no control over the text wrap and layout.

Another method that is very popular in professional websites today is setting the page to a set size. This way, we as the designers have more control over the layout and the results are more predictable. This is the method that we are going to use here.

The next question is what size will we be designing for? Currently the most common target size is 800x600 pixels. Very few people are using resolutions less than that and we can now regard this as the minimum. While resolutions higher than 800x600 are fairly common (at the time of writing entry-level on a new PC is 1024x768), many people will also view the web with a window that's not maximized, so keeping the page looking good at 800x600 is a good practice.

So, having decided to use 800x600 as the target screen size, we have to think about the space taken by toolbars etc. A safe size to start with is 775x410. (Of course, you may wish to design for a different resolution so choose the appropriate size for your target resolution.) The reason we use 775 is to allow 25 pixels for the web browser window and features like the scroll bar that hog screen real estate. As for the height, this is the same formula. We'll have the toolbars and status bars to deal with and these can take up considerable space. You can actually design a page that is higher, (and in many cases you will – a vertically scrolling website is perfectly acceptable). You'll just have to keep in mind that the 410 pixels could be all the viewer sees, so all the important information should fit into this size, especially the navigation of the site. One of the deadly sins of web design is for the viewer to have to scroll to find navigation.

Building the mock-up

1. Create a new document in Photoshop using RGB mode and a resolution of 72 dpi. All images in a web page should be presented in RGB mode and the standard resolution for monitors is 72 dpi.

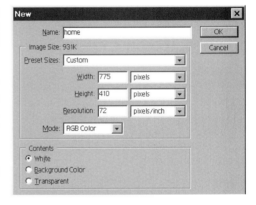

2. Now we need to define the regions. When your new document opens press CTRL/CMD+R to display the rulers. Make sure your units are set to pixels. You can do this easily by right-clicking on the ruler and choosing Pixels from the drop-down list.

3. Using the Move Tool, click and drag on the rulers to drag out the layout guides.

You can see in the illustration the different regions on the page. Make sure you leave at least 60 pixels for the top banner if you wish to use a standard sized banner on your page. A standard banner is 468x60. These are normally used for advertising. The practice of banner advertising is dying fast because viewers have now developed 'banner blindness'. This simply means that viewers have learned to ignore banners without even looking at them, much like receiving spam (unsolicited junk mail).

A page isn't limited to a top or left navigation, but these are the most common so we'll be using them in this example.

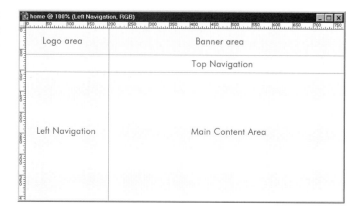

4. Create two new layers for the top and left navigation and name them accordingly.

5. Select the left layer and make a selection with the Rectangular Marquee Tool around the area that will be the left navigation area. Turning on the Snap to Guides feature under the View menu will help in the accuracy of the placement of the selection.

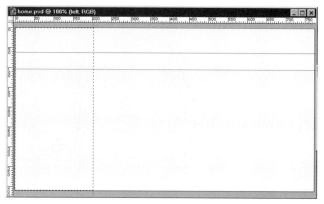

6. Double click on the Foreground Color icon to open the Color Picker

7. Check the websafe color box to limit the display to the 216 websafe color palette. Choose gray #333333.

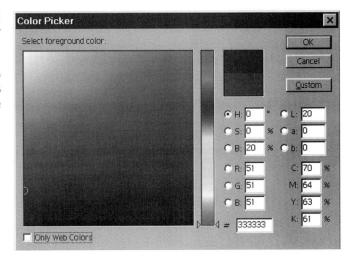

The websafe color palette has been around for quite a while now. It consists of the 216 colors that are common to different operating systems and should be able to reproduce colors that can be displayed on monitors of 256 colors. Although most monitors are running 32,000 or 16 million colors, the palette is still useful because each color has a corresponding hexadecimal number. The number is useful because we can use it to produce consistent color between Photoshop and Dreamweaver. We'll be using this system in the following chapters. You'll see the hexadecimal number in the color picker in Photoshop. It's the 6 digit display beside the # symbol.

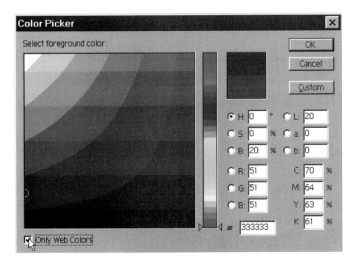

---

8. Fill the selection with the gray color.

9. Using the Rectangular Marquee Tool again, make a selection around the top banner area and select top from the Layers palette.

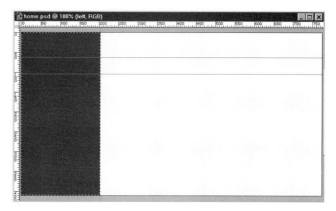

10. Choose a nice light blue color: #6699CC. You can type the numbers directly into the hexadecimal # field to obtain the correct color.

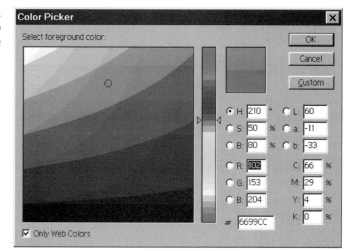

11. Fill the top layer with the color.

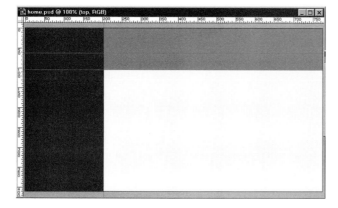

12. You may have to rearrange the layer order for the blue to be on top.

This is a great starting place when you're designing a website. I would even save a copy of this as a base template to save time in the future.

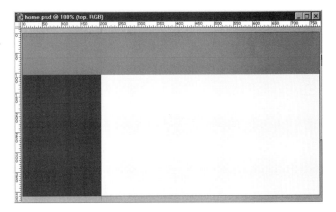

13. We'll be creating a navigation bar on the top section. The buttons are going to be placed under the banner area. We'll want to have a bit of a space between the banner and the buttons on the navigation bar, so drag out another guide. There's no formula for the size you choose - eyeball it. We'll want just enough space to keep the elements from overlapping. I've made the guides black in the screenshot here so you can see where I've placed mine.

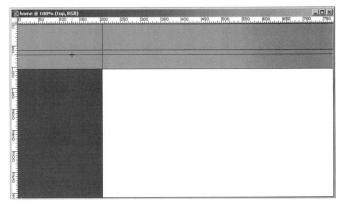

Creating some simple buttons

1. Choose the same gray that we used for the left navigation area as the foreground color for our buttons. If necessary, use the Eyedropper Tool to sample it from the side nav.

2. Select the Rounded Rectangle Tool – it's nested on the toolbar under the Rectangle Tool.

3. Use similar settings to those shown here. There are three options for the type of shape on the toolbar; they are (from left) Shape layers, Paths and Fill pixels (pixel data). I've chosen pixel data because this will produce a filled region that's easy to manipulate later. You could alternatively use a shape layer if you prefer.

4. Create a new layer and name it button.

5. Drag out your mouse on the area you want to turn into a button. You'll see a hint of the shape as you're dragging.

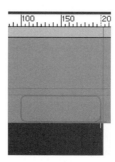

6. As soon as you let go of the mouse your area should be filled. If it isn't, press CTRL/CMD+Z (undo), look at the settings screenshot again and set up your toolbar the same.

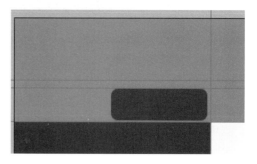

7. Position the new layer where you want your button navigation to start.

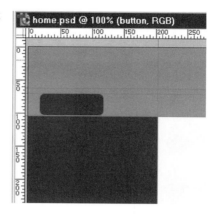

An easy way to duplicate and align elements on a page

1. Select the Move Tool. Hold down the ALT/OPTION key, then begin dragging on your button layer. This will create a duplicate of the object. You'll notice a double arrow. This indicates that you're creating a copy of the layer and not merely moving it. Holding down the SHIFT key at the same time will constrain the movement to a horizontal or a vertical alignment.

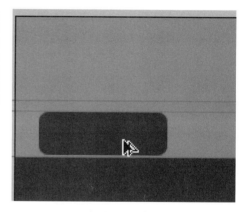

2. Position your new button to suit. You may want to go vertical or you could choose horizontal. In this instance I'm going to make a horizontal toolbar of six buttons.

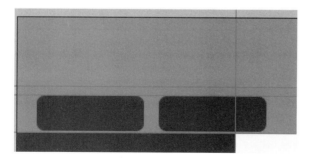

3. Drag out four more copies to make a total of six. Don't worry about perfect spacing or alignment - Photoshop is going to do this for us. The only thing that's important is the placement of the left and the right buttons. We're going to use the Align and Distribute feature to evenly space the others between them.

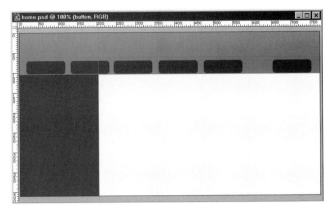

4. Link all the button layers by clicking on the left of the thumbnails. You will see the chain icons to indicate they are linked.

5. With the Move Tool selected, you'll see the Align/Distribute buttons in the toolbar.

6. Choose Align top edges and Distribute horizontal centers.

> When your mouse hovers over the buttons for a few seconds, the tool tips will tell you what each icon does. The names are very self-explanatory. To use this toolbar you must link the layers. The linked layers and only the linked layers will be affected. You may also use the menu if you're unsure of the buttons: Layer > Align Linked *and* Layer > Distribute Linked.

Notice that all the buttons are evenly spaced now? That eliminates a lot of guesswork and slashes the layout time.

Adding text to the buttons

A button isn't too much use unless you tell the user what it will do. We're going to use text in this example. When you're naming buttons, it's best to use a short descriptive name. I've seen some people use very cryptic names on their buttons. While interesting and creative, it doesn't really help the viewer when they don't really know where the button will take them. This makes for bad navigation and you'll lose visitors very quickly with the 'novelty approach'.

1. Choose the Horizontal Type Tool.

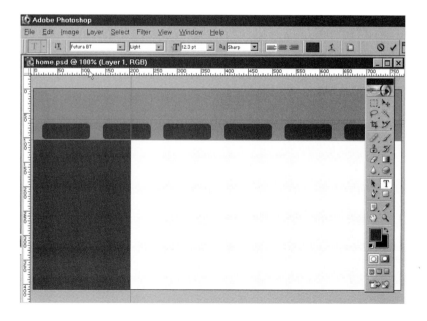

2. Let's select white as the color. Not very exciting, but easy to read, and we do want the viewers to be able to read the labels on our buttons, right?

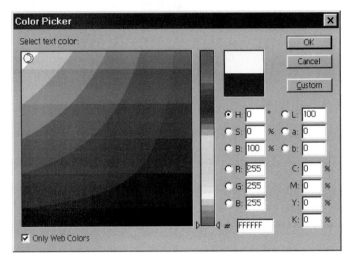

3. Select a nice readable font (yes, I'm a fanatic about readability). My favorite is Futura.

> *Futura is similar to the common Arial and Helvetica. These fonts are good because they're very clean and simple, making them a good choice for onscreen readability. They're called 'sans-serif' ('sans' meaning without) because they contain no serifs. Serifs are the little flicks found on the ends of the letters in fonts such as Times New Roman. The serif was developed to ease readability for typeset body text. The serifs will smoothen out words and make it seem more fluid to ready large amounts of text. However, because of the lower resolution of the screen, the serifs can get cluttered and make legibility more difficult.*

4. Choose a lighter face – a bold type at a small size doesn't usually look good, nor is it clean enough at small sizes. I chose 10 as the point size. A new level of anti-aliasing is available in Photoshop 7 called 'Sharp'. Please use this for all the text on your page.

> *Anti-aliasing is when Photoshop blurs the edges to create a smoother transition between two colors. On smaller fonts, it can make it difficult to read and that's why we have different levels available. 'Smooth' is the softest, but also the blurriest. 'Sharp' or 'None' is the best choice for very small text.*

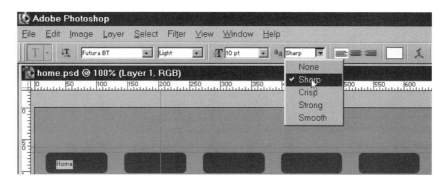

Experiment with your fonts. The medium weight still looks good and is more readable than the light, so this is my choice here. Weights refer to how bold a font face is. A lighter weight is a thinner font and a heavier weight is a bolder face.

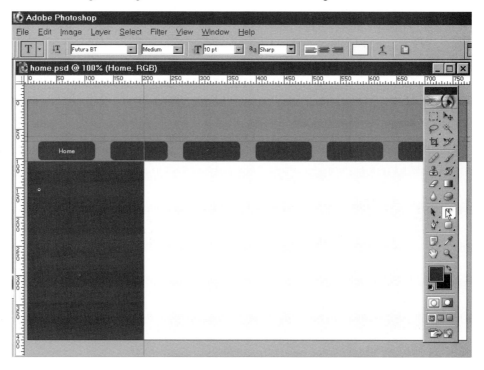

Another trick to make type more readable at smaller sizes is to increase the tracking. This means putting more space between the letters. To demonstrate this, have a look at a street sign or road sign next time you go outside and you'll notice that the type is set with a large tracking to make it easy to read at a glance.

Here's our toolbar with labels on each of the buttons. Notice how clean and readable they look even at a small size? This is our goal.

5. Just as we did with the buttons, link the text layers.

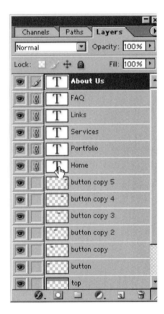

6. We'll align and distribute them like the buttons, using the same technique. You may need to unlink the button text and manually center them in each button. Hold down the SHIFT key to constrain to horizontal movements when you do.

Here we have our navigation bar. It's very simple right now, but we're going to jazz it up a bit later. First we want to organize our layers. You may have noticed that we have a lot of layers already.

Organizing layers

A great feature that came along with Photoshop 6 was layer sets. This allows us to tuck all the layers away into nice snug folders on the layers palette.

1. Select one of the text layers and ensure all the text layers are linked.

2. Click on the arrow at the top right of the toolbar to open the drop-down box. Select New Set From Linked.

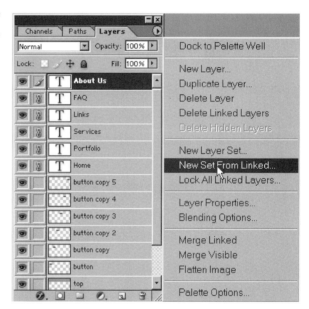

3. Name the set button text.

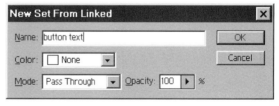

Notice that the text layers are all in a collapsible folder now. You can add or remove layers from the set by simply dragging them. Layer sets can also be ordered on the layers palette by dragging.

4. Choose one of our linked button layers and repeat the last step. This time name the set buttons.

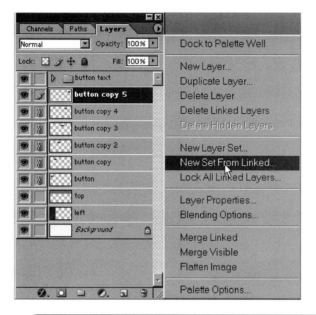

> See how much more organized the Layers palette looks now. This is very important when you're working with many layers. Keep it organized as you go and you will save a lot of hide-and-go-seek later on.

5. We have a slight problem. The text is now hidden. This has only happened because the buttons set was made after the button text set and it's Photoshop's practice to always put the newest set on top. Drag the button text set above the buttons set if the text is no longer visible.

Ah, much better! See how flexible layer sets are? They really come in handy later on for organizing rollovers. Layer sets will save you having to hunt through the layers trying to find the correct one, since they will be organized into manageable sets.

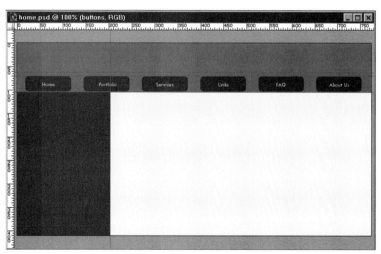

> *If you click on the little arrow next to the set it will expand and reveal all the nested layers.*

Another way we could have laid out the site is with a vertical toolbar, more commonly know as **Left Nav**:

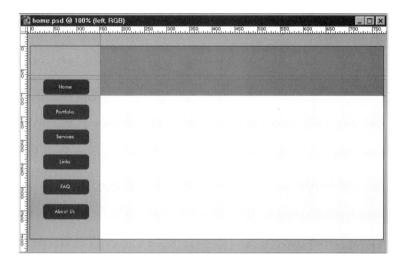

Adding depth to the buttons

The buttons look very clean but they're a bit boring. Let's make our whole page look better now, starting with the buttons. We can give them a de-bossed look.

> *We're going to use some layer styles now to create the look we're after. We'll take a more extensive look at creating buttons with layer styles later on in the book.*

1.   Select one of the button layers.

2.   Click the 'f' icon at the bottom left of the Layers palette and a list of styles will pop up.

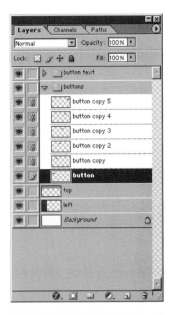

3.   Select Inner Shadow.

The Layer Style dialog box will now open.

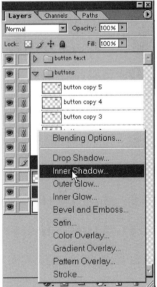

You can apply multiple effects to each style by checking its box and then clicking on its name to modify it. You can also launch the Layer Style dialog box by double clicking the layer thumbnail.

2

4. At this point just use the inner shadow with the settings shown. You can see the effect it's having on the button. Click OK to apply it.

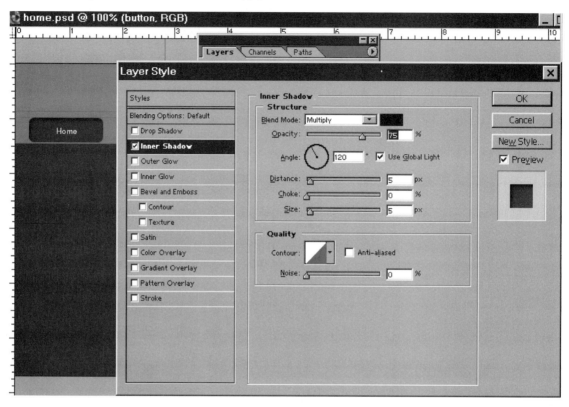

Mass-producing the layer style

You don't have to create the layer style for each layer. You can drag and drop layer styles to any layer and they will instantly take on the same properties. But there is an even faster way to effect multiple layers.

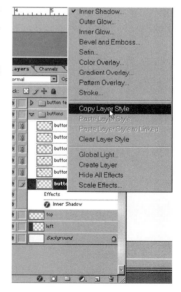

1. Right click on the effects area of the layer (in the Layers palette) and select Copy Layer Style. This will copy all the settings into memory.

2. All the button layers should still be linked. If not, then re-link them.

3. Right-click again and this time select Paste Layer Style to Linked. Of course, we could have copied the layer styles by clicking and dragging the layer style to each layer, but that would have taken a lot more time.

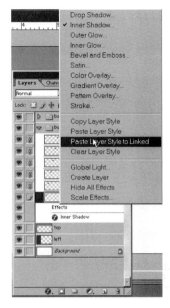

Look at that! In two clicks all the buttons have the inner shadow on them.

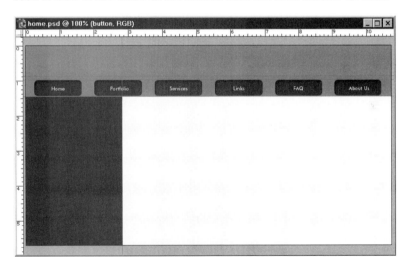

Designing the top part of the page

We're now going to design the top part of the web page. This area is what's going to be seen on the entire site, so it's important to make it look good, but not distracting.

1. First we'll separate the banner area from the toolbar. Create a new layer and name it banner.

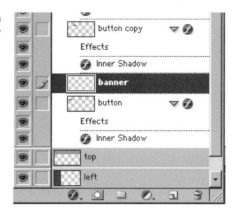

2. Make a selection around the banner area with the Rectangular Marquee Tool.

3. Choose a different color, or in this case a darker shade of the same color. This will make for a smoother design look. I chose #003366 – dark blue.

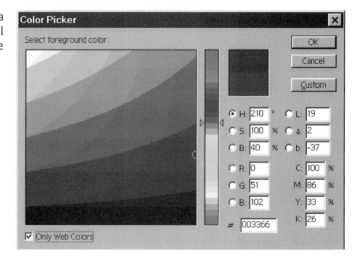

4. Fill the banner area with the new color.

We're now going to make the button area look more polished by adding a highlighted area. This will make it look less flat and give it a shiny rounded look. We're going to do this with gradients, so you can see a different way of applying special effects other than layer styles. Use this same technique to create buttons. For more options and ideas see *Photoshop Most Wanted* also published by friends of ED.

5. Create a new layer called highlight and drag it right under all the buttons, keeping it in the buttons layer set for good house keeping.

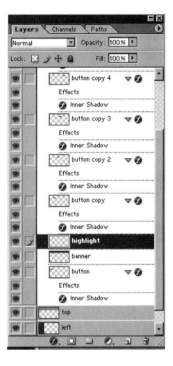

6. Make a selection around the button area. We'll refer to this region as the nav area from now on.

7. Select white as the foreground color. The background color is not important at this time.

8. Select the Gradient Tool. Use Linear Gradient with the Foreground to Transparent setting. Make sure that Transparency is checked in the toolbar too.

9. To apply a gradient click and drag the mouse, you will see a 'path' line. When you release the mouse button the gradient will be applied. CTRL+Z may be a good friend of yours the first few times you try this. Try to get the gradient running halfway up the nav area and white at the top.

Hold the shift key to constrain the gradient to 90 degrees.

10. When you're satisfied with the result, press CTRL/CMD+D to deselect.

11. Press CTRL/CMD+T to enter free transform mode. We're going to shrink the gradient down a little and then blur it to give it softer edges.

12. Drag the handles on the bounding box that will appear to scale the layer. Drag the bottom up halfway and bring the top down just a tiny bit, also bring the sides in a little. Press the ENTER key to apply.

13. Select Filter > Blur > Gaussian Blur. Add a 1-pixel blur to the gradient and press OK.

Here's the result. The nav bar now has a lot more depth to it and now appears rounded on the top.

14. We're now going to stylize the bottom of the nav bar. Create a new layer and name it strip – make sure you place it above the highlight layer. We're going to create a 3D bar across the page.

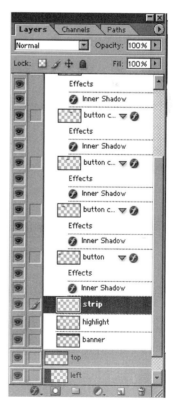

15. Using the Rectangular Marquee Tool, make a thin selection around the bottom of the nav area.

16. Sample the light blue color from the current nav using the Eyedropper Tool. It will be set as the Foreground Color.

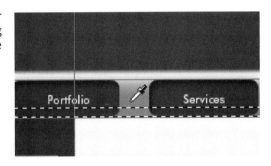

17. If it isn't already, drag the strip layer above the buttons set.

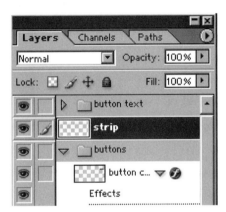

18. Fill with the blue color.

19. Deselect and use Free Transform (CTRL/CMD+T) to make the line thinner if you need to.

20. Open the Layer Style box as we did before by pressing the 'f' icon at the bottom of the Layers palette.

21. Select Bevel and Emboss. Use the settings shown. Also click on Drop Shadow to apply a default shadow to the bar. Click OK.

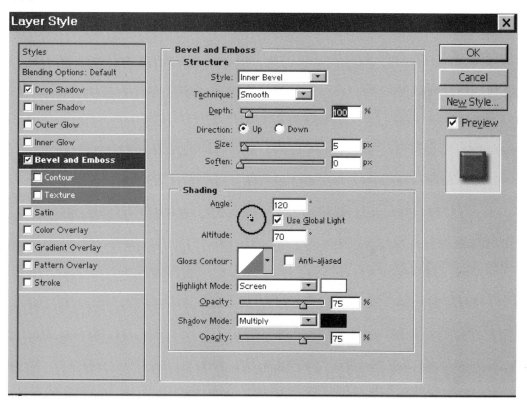

Here's our toolbar now:

22. Press CTRL/CMD+H to hide the guides and take a look to see how we're progressing. If you want a very clean look skip the next step. If you haven't already done so, save your image. Actually, I save almost every time I change something that I want to keep.

Adding some random tone and texture

If you don't like everything looking too perfect and want to add some random looking shadows and highlights with a little bit of texture, here's one of my favorite techniques.

1. Open any 'contrasty' picture in Photoshop. It really doesn't matter what picture you use. Here's one of the sample images that ships with Photoshop. You can find it in the `Photoshop > Samples` directory:

2. Rotate the image so that it's wider than it is long.

3. Now just click on the image area, hold the mouse button and drag the image into our web document.

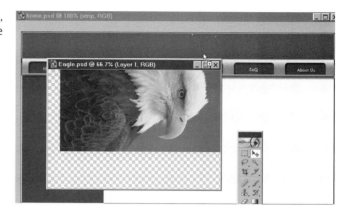

Here's the image in the document:

4. Reposition and scale the image to fill the top area. It doesn't matter how distorted the image becomes. We're making sure that it fits the horizontal width - the height will be trimmed later.

5. Now apply a crazy motion blur by selecting Filter > Blur > Motion Blur. Set the angle to 0. The distance will be entirely dependent on the image used. We're looking for some nice streaks and don't want the image to be recognizable.

Here's our result so far:

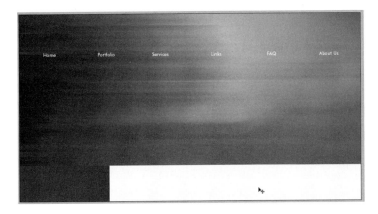

6. We just want the tones of the image and not the color, so change it to Luminosity mode in the top left of the Layers palette.

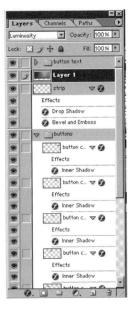

7. Time to trim. Make a selection around the top area.

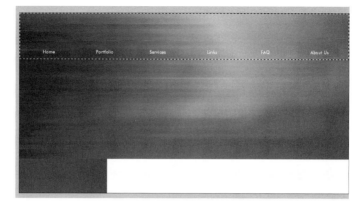

8. Invert the selection by pressing CTRL/CMD+SHIFT+I.

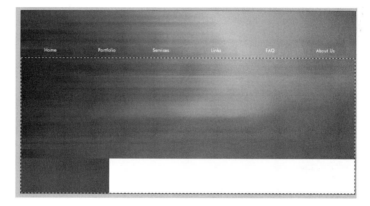

9. Press DELETE to delete everything except for the top area.

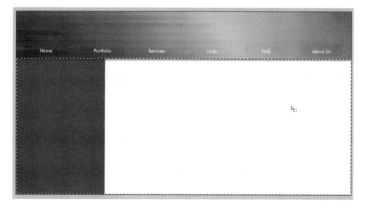

4. Select white as the foreground color.

5. Choose the settings shown here on the toolbar and click on the shapes box for a list of available layer shapes. Click the little arrow on the corner to add more shapes to the library if they're not already visible. Select Add Shapes and navigate to the (Photoshop > Presets > Custom Shapes) directory. You can also just select the shape libraries that are available at the bottom of the Add menu. I chose an animal's footprint called Dog Print from the list.

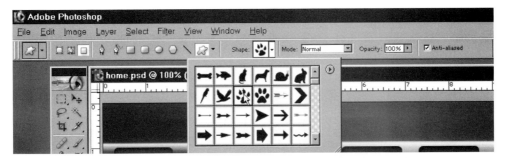

6. Drag the shape onto your page. We're using the Fill pixels option on the top menu bar. Hold down the SHIFT key to keep its proportions correct.

7. Let go of the mouse button and the shape will be applied.

8. It sometimes looks good to drop the opacity a little and blend things in for a more classy look.

9. Add some orange type to the logo.

10. Now add a little yellow type. Notice the two type styles are very different. This produces a better-looking design. We've used contrasting fonts and sizes. Either make them exactly the same or totally different. Two elements that look almost alike don't generally contrast each other to produce a crisp design. The colors are close enough to complement each other – they're right next to each other on the color wheel.

Adding speed lines

1. Let's make your design a bit more trendy with some speed lines. Create a new layer – place it just below the logo layers and name it lines.

2. On the toolbar choose the Line Tool. It's nested under the Custom Shape Tool we just used.

3. Choose 1 pixel for the width and select the Fill pixels option. Choose white as the foreground color.

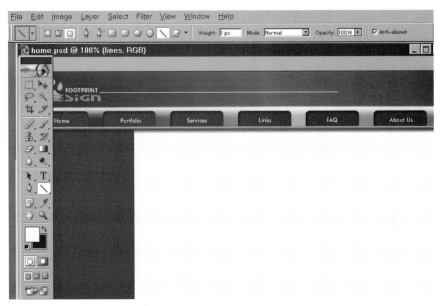

4. Drag the Line Tool (holding down the SHIFT key to constrain the angles). I added three line segments all on the same layer. Don't overdo it.

5. Select Filter > Blur > Motion Blur. Apply a large motion blur to the lines at the same angle the lines run.

See how it tapers the ends off and adds a pleasing result:

6. Let's drop the opacity down some, to blend the effect into the page a bit more. Use the Opacity selector in the Layers palette as shown in the screenshot.

7. Now add some text to the banner area. We'll add an actual banner in a later chapter.

8. You could also add some text for the 'Contact Us' link. We'll make this an **image map** in an upcoming chapter. The arrows are just more custom shapes on separate layers and at different opacities.

Notice how I'm decorating the banner area. You can decorate yours however you like; we're just using the same techniques that we've learned in this chapter so far. The top area is complete. Part of good design is knowing when to stop. It's easy to get carried away and overdo a design and ruin it. Simplicity is still a very strong design element.

The main content area

The nav bar is now complete and this is the most important part of the design. We're going to lay out the content area, but this is just a mock up with 'dummy' content to give the client an idea of how the pages will be laid out. The text we use will be replaced by HTML text when we go into Dreamweaver. HTML is much faster loading and way easier to update.

We could try adding a gradient to the background to see how it looks. I used the same blue and gray from the nav for the gradient. Notice I reuse a lot of colors again and again? That's another principle of design - the repeating elements give an integrated and together look. If I were to choose too many colors, the design would be too busy.

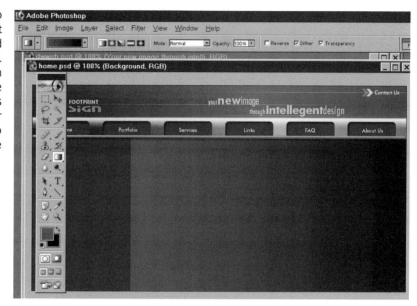

You can be too busy with color, layout, fonts and images. Try not to clutter your designs and they will look a lot more professional. Understanding all the elements that go into a design will help you to use them with each other. There will be times when you'll use a lot of color. These are good times to generally limit the use of other elements or once again we'll fall into the clutter syndrome. This is the beauty of the mock-up; if the client doesn't like it, we can easily change it.

Adding some dummy content

We're going to create some dummy content. This content may or not be the same in the final page. It's intended as an example of what the page design will look like with some content. The content usually ends up totally different in my experience. I sometimes link the dummy content together and reuse it for different page designs just to save time. It's good to use an image that's relevant to the subject to help 'sell' the design.

1. Add a header to the content area. Again, no weird fonts here. We just want simple, clean fonts to match the look of the page. I wish I had the space to talk more about font usage, but that's a whole book on its own. In a nutshell, try to use fonts that match your design. Also, remember that common fonts like Arial, Times, Courier and Verdana will be installed on many computers, so these fonts can be adapted as HTML text once we convert the mock up into an HTML page. In most cases never use more than three fonts on a design and vary the sizes and weights. But don't have too many variations on one page, unless that's the look you're really after.

2. Add a little dummy text to your page. I've used Latin text that really doesn't say anything – it's just placeholder text to show the client what the page would look like with some text on it. The fact that it's in Latin will prevent the client from being distracted by what it says – unless he knows Latin, of course!

3. You could try dropping in an image for flavor. Just drag and drop like we did with the eagle image and scale to fit.

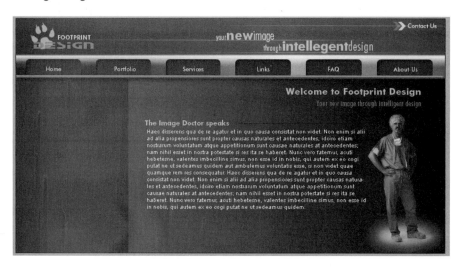

4. I added an image and some text to the left part of the page to balance the design.

5. Let's add a box at the bottom of the page. This will work with the large area at the top and bring more balance to the page layout. Create a new layer and call it callbox.

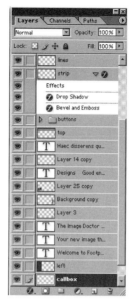

6. Drag out a rectangle selection that lines up with the left of the text.

7. Fill with the same gray as we used on the left.

8. Apply some more text to the box.

> *Notice how the text contrasts, but also matches the look of the page. Everything should be adding to a strong design and not taking away from it with a total style break*

9. Now we'll create some different buttons for the side nav area. Create a layer called side button.

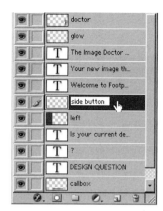

10. Select the Rounded Rectangle Tool.

11. Use the settings as shown.

12. Drag out a rounded rectangle.

13. Add a bevel as shown.

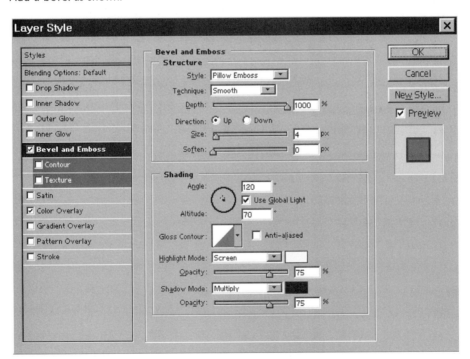

14. Also, add a color overlay, choosing the settings shown.

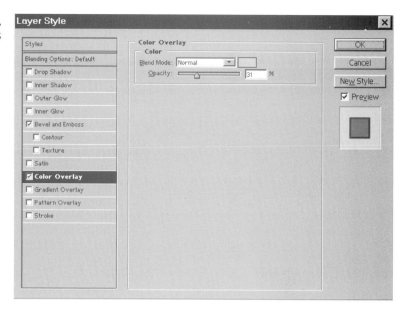

15. Here's the result – different looking pill shaped buttons:

16. Add some text to our buttons and we're almost good to go.

17. For a finishing touch I added a bigger footprint behind the text with the Custom Shape Tool. Did I overdo it? Let's show it to the client and find out.

Summary and what's coming next

We've now created a mock-up of a web page. You could save it as a JPG file and e-mail to your client for approval or changes. You'll find it's a lot easier to decide on a final design now and make any changes before you start building the page itself.

In the next chapter we're going to take this design and actually turn it into a working web page. We'll be using the Slice and Rollover Tools in Photoshop and ImageReady. We'll also be going into image optimization in depth so that your page will download quickly from the Internet.

We have considered some sound web design rules and decided on our main look and feel. We have looked at creating a mock-up of a web page. Once the design has been approved it's time to take that mock-up and turn it into a fully functioning website. The good news is that we don't have to start from scratch, we already have the framework for our site designed!

This chapter is going to teach you how to transform our mock-up and turn it into an HTML document that's ready to use in Dreamweaver.

We are going to look at **slicing**, **optimizing**, creating **rollover effects** and **exporting** the whole lot for use in Dreamweaver MX. Along the way, you're going to learn some useful site planning principles. In this chapter we will use some Photoshop, but will predominantly be using ImageReady.

Slicing explained

The goal of a website ranges widely, from selling a product, creating PR, announcing events, showcasing a new invention to marketing a whole new company. The goal of web design, however, is always the same; to create a fast loading, visually interesting site that is easy to navigate and communicates the message clearly. One of the pieces to this puzzle is the **slice**.

Slicing an image is simple in theory. We will take one large image and break it into lots of smaller images, like a jigsaw puzzle, and reassemble the pieces seamlessly in a web page using HTML layout tables.

We'll need to be intuitive in deciding how and where to add the slices; there are two things to keep in mind when planning them:

- We will want to keep the number of slices to a minimum. This way they will be easier to manage.

- When we make buttons, it's a good idea to carefully align them. Even a slight error in alignment could throw things off and cause problems later on.

There are a whole range of reasons why slicing is a good idea. Here are the main advantages:

- You can turn slices into buttons or 'hot' areas.
- You can mix optimization methods, meaning your sliced image will download faster than it would have as one single image (more on this later in this chapter).
- You can replace portions of an image with other images or even HTML text areas.
- You can reuse elements of a design utilizing the browser's cache.
- Animations can be created and inserted into small areas and be seamlessly integrated into the design.
- Placeholder slices can later be used to house other objects such as Macromedia Flash movies.

- It makes re-skinning a site later easier. You will have all the guides laid out for the redesign, you can use the same slices, allowing you to export the new images over the top of the old ones. This is mainly useful when you have a standard design that you want to customize for different customers, and may want to re-brand each version slightly. This technique can also be used if you want to have several 'themes' for the website that the user can switch between.

Slicing our mock-up

Now let's assume the example from the last chapter went to the client and they said, "I love the design, but I don't want the footprint on the background or the gradient. Just use a dark blue background for the pages. Also I don't want the gray box on the bottom. Everything else is good to go, build the site." This is very realistic to what a client may say in the real world. With those instructions, we will proceed to build the sample site. Remember you can still follow along using your own original design if you like.

Open the document in Photoshop.

You will see the Slice tool in the Tools palette.

Click and hold on the tool to reveal the Slice Select tool. The functions are just like the names imply. The Slice tool is used to create slices and the Slice Select tool is used to make a slice active for editing. We are going to explore several methods of slicing. The method you choose is totally dependent upon your document and your preferred workflow. However, there are various situations that lend themselves to certain methods. We will slice our page using this assortment of methods and use the best one for each purpose.

Slices From Guides

When the Slice tool is selected, the toolbar at the top will reflect the options for this tool. You will see an option that says Slices from Guides. This is the simplest and quickest of all the slicing options. If you used guides to help you lay out the page, press this button and the image will be sliced right on these guides. You may want to strategically add some guides before using this method.

Here you can see the slices created by the guides. Notice each slice is depicted by a box and a number in the top left. A number is automatically assigned each time you create a slice. This helps to identify each small image that will be created. The number will be added to its file name at the output stage.

As you can see here, the slice from guide doesn't encompass all our needs, but it's a great starting place.

Layer based slices

Another way to create slices is the Layer Based Slice option. Layer based slices are the most intelligent slices, because of the integrated features in Photoshop 6+. This method is excellent for buttons and creates a slice around the content of any given layer and provides the following advantages:

- When the image on the layer is resized, the layer-based slice automatically resizes to match.

- When you move the content of the layer, the slice will move with it.

- When you are creating rollovers the layer will be automatically selected in the Layers palette.

To create a layer based slice, highlight the layer to slice by clicking on it in the Layers palette. Begin with the first button layer on the example.

In the Layers menu choose New Layer Based Slice.

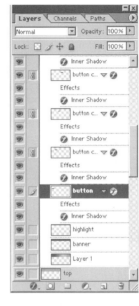

That's it! See the slice added to the first button on our nav bar.

Notice how the slice tracks with the layer if I move it? This only works with the layer based slices.

User defined slices

These are the meat and potatoes slices. Nothing fancy about these. They are created manually and are probably the most common type you will use.

Choose the Slice tool and click and drag like you would with the Marquee tool. Watch the edges very carefully when doing this to make sure the slices are accurate; you can use guides to help and also switch to the Slice Select tool to make minor adjustments later if you need to touch up your slices.

> *Untidy slices will make your final HTML web page unnecessarily complicated and lead to larger file sizes. Try to line slice edges up neatly to avoid extra unwanted complexity.*

A user slice on the image.

Taking it to ImageReady

To launch ImageReady click the big button at the bottom of the tool palette. This will launch ImageReady and transfer all your image data over.

After a few moments (or a bit longer depending on your system resources!), ImageReady will launch and you will see your page with all the slices intact. You can press the same button again to go back to Photoshop at any time. Any changes made in Photoshop or ImageReady will be reflected in the master document. When you save from either program all the settings will be retained.

You will notice that the interface for ImageReady is similar to Photoshop but there are a few new features, like optimized display, rollovers, image maps and animation features.

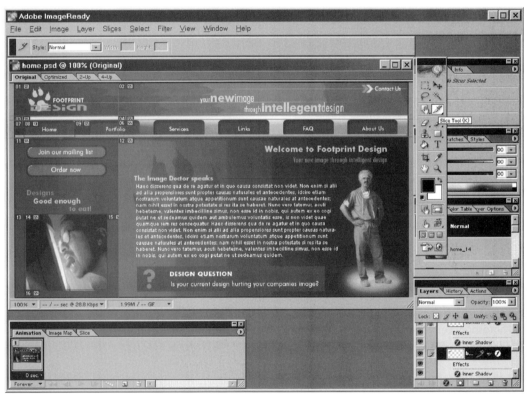

3

The tool to use is the Slice Select tool.

We have three slices on the banner area of our page. Let's combine them into one! There is really no problem with the three slices, but we're combining them in order to demonstrate the merging technique. It will also be easier for you to work with in the coming chapters.

Click on the first slice using the Slice Select tool. Hold down the SHIFT key and click on the next one. Notice that both slices are now selected.

Hold down the SHIFT key and click on the third. There are now 3 slices selected.

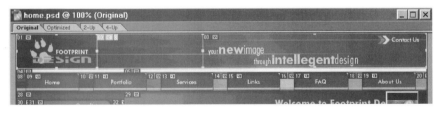

Choose Slice > Combine Slices.

Now all 3 are combined into one. All the other numbers and slice names are automatically updated.

Previewing our page

Here is a view of our web page showing just the slices. See how they are positioned intelligently, aligned into rows and columns. Since HTML tables will be built to hold the slices (a separate cell for each image), we want to keep the number of table rows and columns to a minimum.

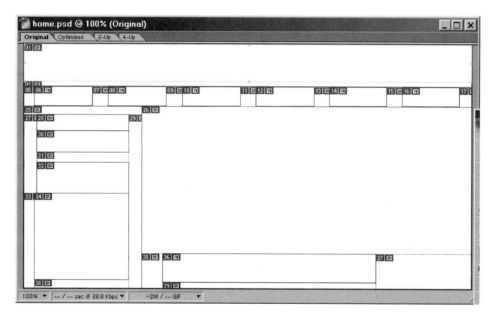

7. In the Color Overlay dialog box, a list of websafe colors will appear. You can also choose the foreground or background colors or a custom color. To add a custom color choose Other.

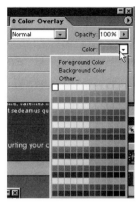

The standard color picker will appear.

8. I chose a lighter gray for our rollover color.

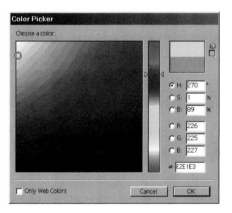

Here is what the button would look like with the rollover.

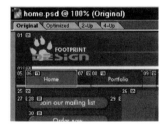

9. To test the rollover press the Preview button or hit CTRL/CMD+ALT/OPTION+P.

10. Hide the slices and move the mouse over the button. It should change and then go back when the mouse is moved away again. Performance will be a bit slower in ImageReady than in your web browser, but the goal here is just to make sure you are satisfied with the effect.

Now go to the Slices palette. You will see a preview of the slice and its name in a field.

11. In the URL field type the name of the link to want to got to when you click the button. You can define an **absolute** (generally this is used to take you to a link on another website) or a **relative** link (this will take you to a different page on the same website).

Absolute: http://www.yourlink.com/here.html.
Relative: somewhere/page023.html.

Adding links at this point is optional. We can always add them later with Dreamweaver.

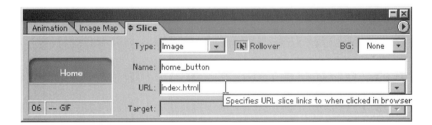

18. Add an Inner Glow layer effect.

19. Use the settings as shown here.

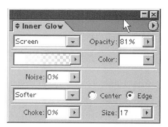

You will see the inner glow on the button.

20. Repeat the effect on the second button.

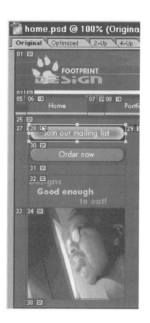

21. Preview the rollover in ImageReady to see how it will work.

Congratulations! You have now learned how to create a variety of different slices and also how to create rollover effects. We will now learn how to optimize our images for displaying on the web.

Optimization

This is one of the techniques that sets the design pro apart from the graphics hack. Optimization is the art of reducing a file's size to the absolute minimum and still retain good image appearance. I have been asked countless times "how can you keep your images looking so sharp and yet have them download so fast?" In this section you will find out. ImageReady has some very powerful optimization tools. By the time you have read this chapter you will be producing sharp images that will download very fast indeed.

Exploring the Optimization window

Notice that there are tabs on the top of the image area. The default is Original; this is the working preview. Once you're ready to optimize the page, the other options will come in handy. We will look at them in order as we work our way through the example web page.

Click on Optimized.

This is the default optimized view. This is what the images are going to look like when your page is optimized. Generally, you will be looking at it a slice at a time. To see the overall impact of the page, click the Hide Slices button.

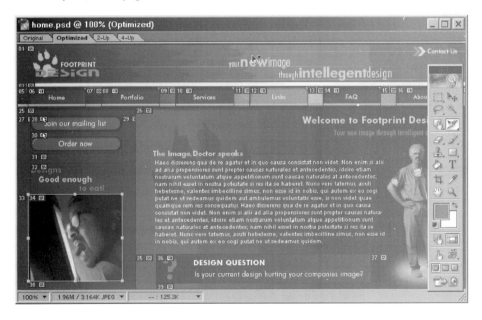

You can customize the display on the status bar at the bottom of the image area. Click and hold the small arrow to see this pop-up menu.

We don't have the space to go through all the settings here, but most of them are self explanatory.

My favorite happens to be download time for the 28k modem. Although almost no one uses this technology anymore, it's a good indication of download time on a 56k modem with heavy traffic on the server. Besides, 56k users rarely get a better connection than 33k due to ISP limitations. The optimized file size will also be displayed next to the download time.

As you can see starting from the left, the original size of the page is 1.96M, the selected slice is 6.06K and it's a GIF. Moving to the right, the default optimized setting is 125.3K and it would take 45 seconds to download on a 28k modem. We will be able to improve the appearance and reduce the file size some more.

Time to optimize a slice. Since we already have the small picture selected, let's begin there. It's currently a GIF and 6.06K. As we learned earlier in the book, GIF is good for text and large smooth areas and JPEG is better for photos.

In the Optimize palette, choose JPEG from the pull-down menu.

Reduce the quality to the lowest before it looks too depreciated. JPEG compression works by throwing away image data. This is known as lossy compression. You can reduce a fair bit before it becomes noticeable. Here we reduced to 30.

See how the image still looks great but its file size is a shade of what it was. We are now weighing in at 3.164K.

2-Up view

The next option on the preview pane is the **2-Up** view. This enables you to compare the original view with the optimized image in a visual manner. In this view you also get more detailed information about your slice.

Notice the window under you optimized view, it tells you the size and download time for the individual slice. You are also informed of the exact settings including number of colors in the GIF, the palette used and the amount of dither used.

> Dithering is when a pattern is created to smoothen out obvious lines where the colors change in a gradient.

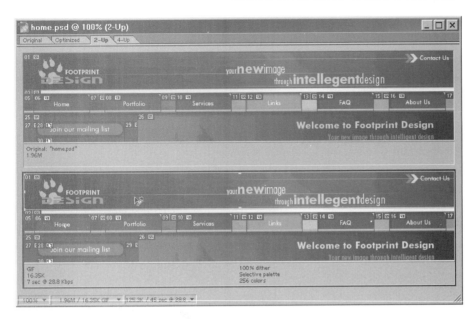

Simply click on another slice to pull up its information.

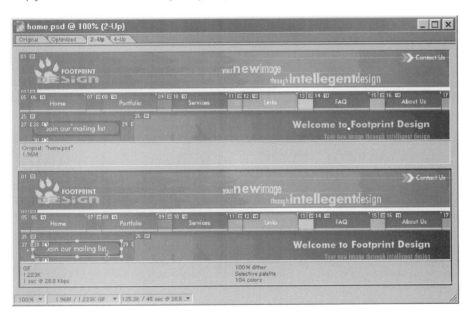

4-Up view

This is the same as the 2-Up except this time you get to compare 3 optimized versions against the original. By default, ImageReady will choose options with cascading qualities. Choose the best one as a starting place and then do your fine-tuning.

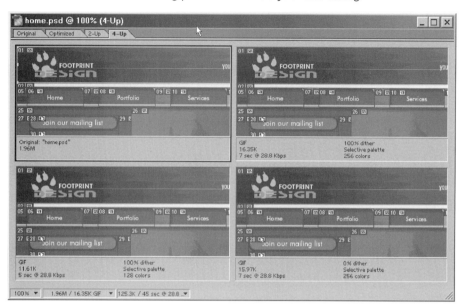

Let's optimize a few slices now.

1. Go back to the 2-Up view; I favor this because I can see more of the image I'm working on. I suggest that you find what works best for you and use that.

2. Looking at the banner area, it's a GIF and over 16K in size.

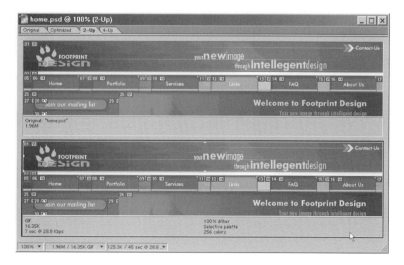

Usually this slice would be an excellent choice for a GIF, but because of the effect on the background, JPEG will work better, so switch to JPEG. You will see that the display says 30 quality – this is because ImageReady will remember the last used setting. The file size is only 6.5K now, but the text is looking a bit blurry.

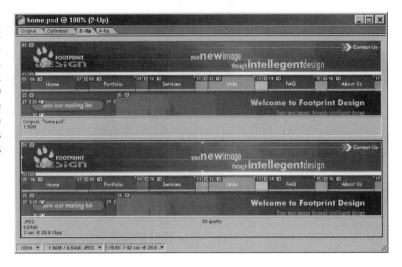

3. Take the quality up until you like the result. Let's try 55.

You shouldn't have to use a higher setting than this, except in a few cases, like a gallery when you want to show an image at its absolute best. Even then, a setting of 70-80 would usually be more than enough.

The text is sharper now and the size is still only 11K. This is still a bit bigger than I would generally use, but I feel it's worth the trade-off to keep the text as sharp as possible.

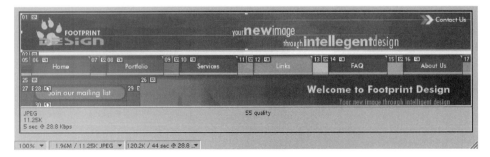

4. Now select the next slice. It's the thin gray line beneath the banner area. Since we are looking at an area of consistent tone and color, choose GIF.

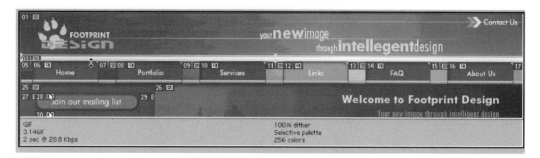

One of the ways that GIFs compress files is by limiting the colors on the palette. You can discard a large number of colors without losing a lot of quality and you can substantially slash the image size.

5. In the Colors pull-down choose 16 colors.

We have gone from over 3000 bytes to 613 bytes – that's a huge saving!

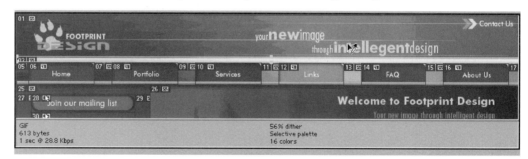

6. Optimize the buttons using 16-color GIFs.

You could get away with using eight colors if it wasn't for the inner shadows, but using too few colors would create banding on the soft edges. Banding is when there is not enough color information to smoothly render a gradient. That is also where dithering comes in. We can add some dither in the optimizing palette to soften those edges. We have used 100% dither here to get the smoothest result.

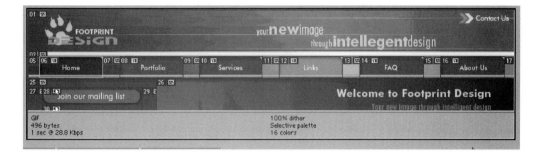

> While in the preview pane, if you need to see a different part of the image, hold the spacebar and drag the image in the window.

7. Go through the rest of the slices and optimize them one at a time until the entire document is optimized.

8. Hide the slices again to view the entire page. Choose the Optimized view and check for any seams that might have occurred because of uneven optimization of adjoining slices. If you see uneven joins, choose the Slice Select tool and make any fixes by resizing the slices.

All the images on the page are now down to 98K. When you realize that the content area is 69.5K itself that is pretty impressive.

> You can get these figures by selecting a slice and looking at its stats in the status bar in ImageReady.

The entire framework for the page is now only approximately 30K. Presently the content area is an image, but we will be replacing it with HTML text and smaller images in Dreamweaver, which we will do in the very next chapter.

Exporting the page

We have now created our basic page and optimized it. Finally we will need to export all the slices and create an HTML page with tables for the slices to be reassembled. You guessed it, ImageReady will create the HTML and JavaScript for us.

Save the PSD document before you do anything; it would be a shame to have a crash and lose your work now! Create a new folder on you hard drive. This is where we are going to export our page to.

File > Save Optimized As…

Find the folder we just created and choose a file name. The HTML document will have this name and so will the sliced images. Click Save.

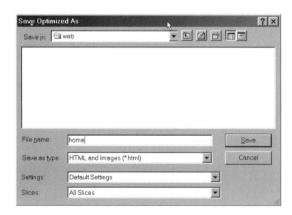

You will see the status bar at the bottom as ImageReady creates the page and exports all the images as slices.

Look in your folder and you will see an HTML document and a folder labeled images.

Open the images folder and you will see all your slices and rollover states as individual images. This is great news if you have ever had to slice images by hand, like I did before Adobe ImageReady came along.

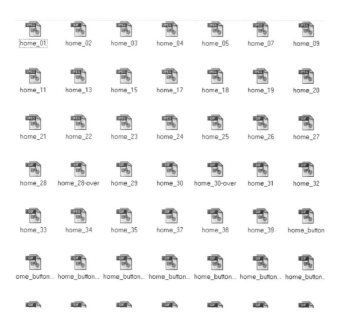

Double click your HTML document to launch it in your web browser.

Check it out and make sure it work and that the rollovers all function correctly. If they don't, go back to ImageReady and troubleshoot. Go through each rollover slice and in the Rollovers palette, test its different states and keep an eye on the main image window. Then preview it in your browser. When you have found the problem, re-export the page and test it again in your browser.

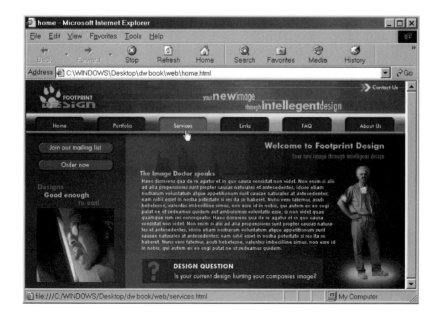

Summary

Congratulations, you have just created a fully functional web page, complete with rollover effects. In the following chapters we are going to add Macromedia Dreamweaver to the equation. You will learn how to really get into the nitty gritty of web design and flesh out our entire site and add content using Dreamweaver. We will return to Photoshop and ImageReady periodically, but from here Dreamweaver will be in the spotlight.

4 Introducing Dreamweaver

In this chapter...

We take a good look at Dreamweaver, the interface and some basic features. We will then see how our ImageReady-exported web page looks when viewed in Dreamweaver, covering along the way:

- The Dreamweaver workspace
- Defining and modifying sites
- Opening pages from ImageReady and modifying them in Dreamweaver
- Creating pages from scratch in Dreamweaver
- Tables, colors, backgrounds and alignment.

In the previous chapters, we've discussed planning our website and have actually designed a working page. We're now going to use Dreamweaver to take this page and turn it into a fully functional website. You'll learn how to define a site, build a site, add features and modifications and then upload the site to the web for viewing. Going into every feature of Dreamweaver is beyond the scope of this book, but by the time you're finished you'll be familiar enough with the main features to feel comfortable building great looking websites in Dreamweaver.

In this chapter you'll learn how to define your site and open your ImageReady page. You'll also learn how to create tables and insert images into the tables to create layouts.

> *When we talk about defining our site, we mean setting up a location on your computer to store the site and its assets. By defining this directory structure you will be able to test most of the features on your computer with all the pieces in place and then upload it all intact onto the web for online viewing.*

First, let's look at the Dreamweaver interface.

The Dreamweaver workspace

When you first launch Dreamweaver MX this is what you'll see:

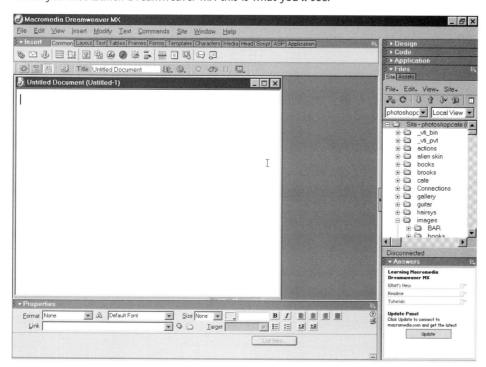

This is the slightly revamped MX layout, but if you're very used to working with Photoshop's layout we can actually revert to the classic layout of Dreamweaver, which features the floating Tools palette we're all used to.

> *This step is totally optional. We are going to mainly work in the classic layout to make it easier to follow along, no matter what version you are used to. The be honest, I prefer to use the classic layout because it's more similar to what I am used to. This is of course totally your preference and doesn't effect the functionality or features in the least.*

Let's change our workspace: Edit > Preferences.

Click on General. Then choose the Change Workspace button.

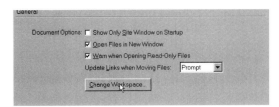

You will be given a choice of the MX or DW4 (classic) Workspace. Choose Dreamweaver 4 if you prefer and click OK.

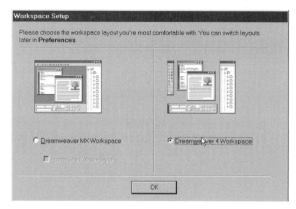

You will now see a dialog box that tells you your change will take effect on the next launch. Close Dreamweaver (I know, seems like we only just opened it!) and restart it.

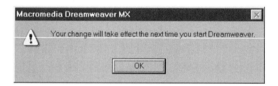

You will now see this layout. Just like in previous versions, everything is floating once again. I love this layout and the flexibility it gives me.

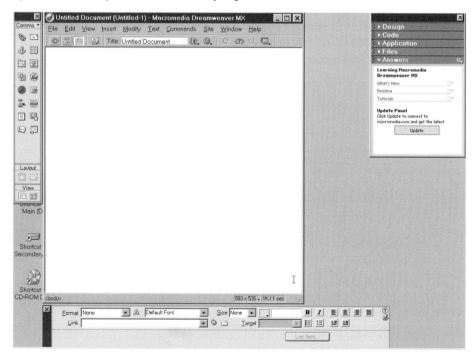

Let's look at it in more depth. The toolbars are at the top left. Under that is the document preview area. This is where you'll see your page as we work on it. At the bottom is the Properties panel (sometimes known as the Property inspector). We'll be using this extensively during the course of the book. To the right you'll see an assortment of other panels. We'll be looking at some of these too.

To reduce screen clutter we can have the launcher buttons displayed on our status bar.

Select Edit > Preferences and choose Panels from the Category menu on the left of the window.

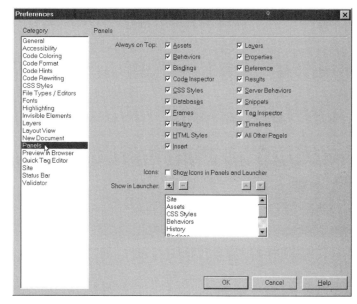

Check the box that says Show Icons in Panels and Launcher.

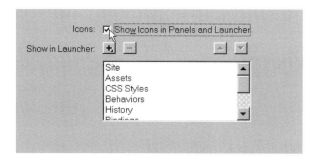

Click OK and look on the bottom right of your window; you'll see a new row of buttons.

From left these are: Site Map, Assets, Cascading Style Sheets, Behaviors, History, Data Bindings, Server Behaviors, Components and Databases. We won't be using the last four features but we will come across the other features as we work our way through the book.

Defining your site

As we discussed, defining a site simply means setting up a local folder for your files and telling Dreamweaver where to find everything. It also involves setting up your remote hosting information; the remote hosting information is simply where you will store your website for online viewing. We'll look at that after we have built the site.

Let's define our site now.

1. Choose Site > New Site.

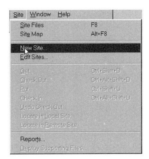

2. There are two options: Basic and Advanced. Click on Basic for now. Dreamweaver will now use a wizard to help you set up your site root.

3. In the first window you should enter the name of your site (I've simply named mine Dreamweaver-site). Click Next.

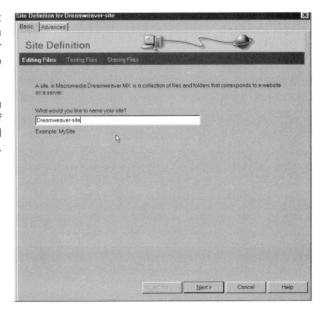

4. This page asks if you want to use a server technology. If we selected Yes, it would enable the use of backend databases and code to make the pages dynamic (database driven). We don't need this functionality so check No. We'll be building our pages in HTML. Click Next.

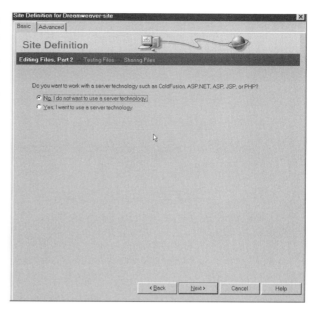

5. On the next screen check the first option; we'll be editing locally. This just means you'll be building your web page on your standalone computer and uploading it to the web when you're finished. This is the most common method used.

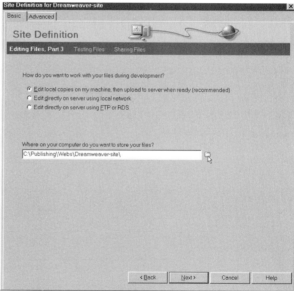

6. Where do you want to store your files? Click the little folder icon to browse for a directory.

7. Find the web folder we created for the ImageReady page we built in the last chapter. If you're starting fresh, just create a folder somewhere on your hard drive. Click Select.

8. For the next step, choose None for now. We'll go back later on and add the server info when we're ready to upload. We'll also do that in Advanced view so that you get the chance to use both methods.

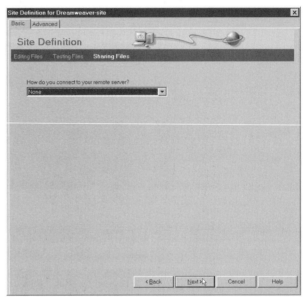

9. Click Next and you'll see a summary page, and Done to proceed and let Dreamweaver set everything up.

10. If you have files in the folder you'll see a cache warning box. Click OK to allow Dreamweaver to set up a cache. This makes files load faster and uses less CPU power.

11. You'll now see your site in the Edit Sites window. As you can see, I also have some other sites set up previously. Click Done.

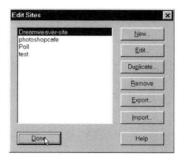

Congratulations, your site is now defined and all your files will be saved to the correct locations when you create your website. The Dreamweaver site window will now open. This is where you can view and manage all the files in your website. It's important that you save all the files to this directory in order for them to work correctly when you upload them to the web server. You can create as many sub directories as you want, as long as they are under your main directory, known as the **root**. If you want to open the site definition feature again, double click the name of your site in the Site drop down.

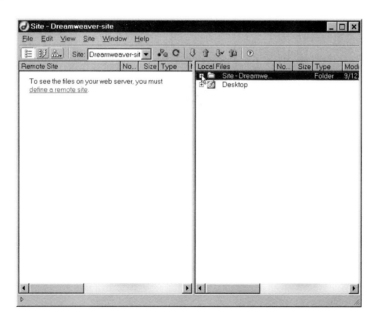

> *Here's the Site Definition window again. This time I've clicked on the Advanced tab. You can see all our settings in their correct boxes. In future you could just skip the wizard and enter the information directly into the advanced setup if you prefer.*

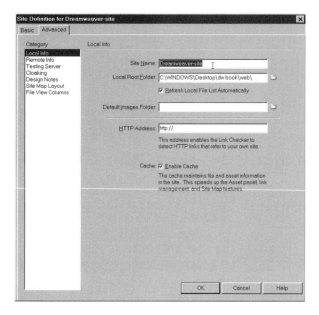

Opening home.html in Dreamweaver

Back to the Site window: the right panel is where all our local information will reside. The left panel is for the remote server.

1. You'll see our `home.html` document that we created in the previous chapter. You'll also notice an images folder that was automatically created. To expand it click the [+] symbol.

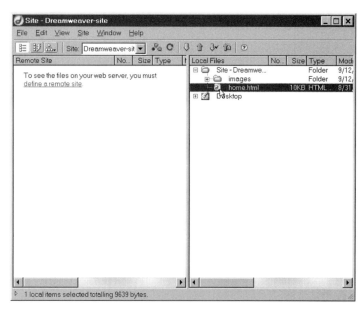

2. You'll now see all your images files. To collapse the view again, press the [–] sign.

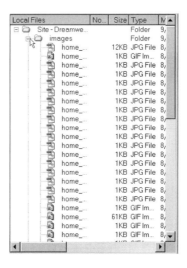

We can also collapse the window to show only the local information. This is good to save screen real-estate while developing your website. The local files are the ones that you create on your computer. The remote files are the same files after they have been moved to the web server.

3. Click the arrow at the bottom left.

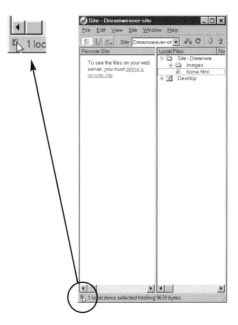

Now only the local folders are showing. If you haven't defined a remote location yet, the default view in MX is to show only the local information. The arrow at the bottom will actually toggle the view between the local only and the dual pane views. To open an HTML document, you only have to double-click on it in the Site window.

4. Double click `home.html`.

Here's our page. Dreamweaver recognizes all the code generated from ImageReady because it's standard HTML.

You'll notice there is a little yellow icon at the start and finish of the page. This is the visual representation to show that there is a hidden element. It won't display on the actual website but it's there to alert you to some information. In this case it's a **comment tag**. A comment is a piece of information that a designer can add about a page and it will be skipped by the browser and not appear on the final page.

> *If you can't see these, then you must choose to show the page's invisible elements:* View > Visual Aids > Invisible Elements.

5. To view the comment, click on it with your mouse.

Look at the Properties panel and the comment will be displayed. In this case it's informing you of the ImageReady slices.

6. Press DELETE to remove the comment tags – this time they're not necessary.

> Note: Don't go deleting these tags every time you see them without checking what they are in the Properties panel first. Some of the tags may be JavaScript or form fields which should not be deleted. Comments can be deleted, but if you leave them, that's OK too, they won't hinder the functionality of the page. In HTML a comment will look like: `<!—comment here — >` The tag tells the browser to skip this particular command and not run any of the code between the `<!— — >` tags. The comments are there to help the designer to remember what a piece of code does or to generally leave some notes for future reference. ImageReady's comments just remind you where its auto-generated code starts and ends.

7. To preview the page in a web browser press F12.

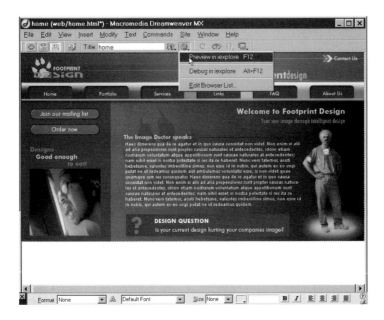

You'll now see our page in Internet Explorer. As you can see, Dreamweaver has recognized the ImageReady design and displayed it accordingly.

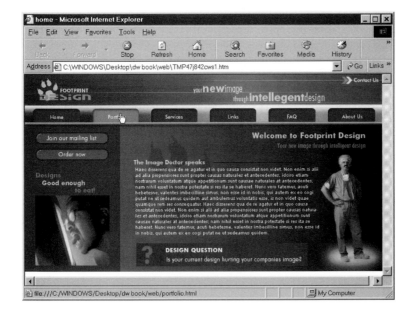

Exploring the workspace some more

Click on an image in Dreamweaver.

The Properties panel will display some info about the image. Under W and H you'll see the dimensions of the image. **Src** will tell you the location and name of the (source) image. The HTML code that Dreamweaver will write will look something like this.

```
<img src=".../images/home_01.jpg" width="775"
➥ height="62">
```

`img src=""` is the HTML that specifies there is an image, the location: (../images/) and the name (home_01.jpg) of the image.

The `width="775"` and `height= "62"` are written by the W and H fields in Dreamweaver.

Here you can see the link when we click on a linked image:

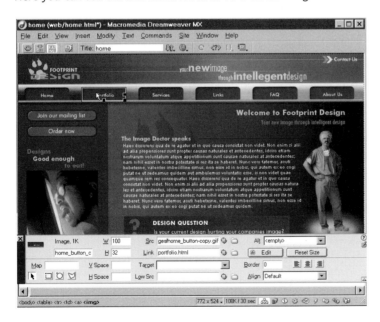

If you click on the first button on the top left of the toolbar (Code view button), you can view the HTML source of the page. As your knowledge of HTML grows, you can edit directly in this window and even write the raw HTML code yourself. I personally like to write the code with Dreamweaver and then open Code view and do some tweaking by hand.

There is a third, split Code/Design view where you can see the visual page and the code at the same time. This is very useful for trouble shooting quickly. You can rest assured, though, that you don't have to know any HTML to build web pages in Dreamweaver.

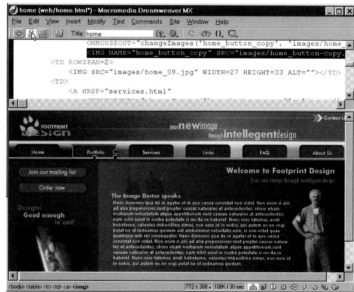

Creating a page in Dreamweaver

Let's reproduce our page from scratch in Dreamweaver. This will be good to help you understand how Dreamweaver and tables work. Up to this point you may still not understand how tables help our design.

A table in web design is a rectangle divided into rows and columns. Each smaller rectangle created by the rows and columns is called a **cell**. Tables were originally designed as containers for text data. Tables are used extensively to lay out web pages because the edges can be made invisible by setting the borders to a value of 0. Because of this, your table doesn't actually have to be visible at all.

The HTML will look something like this, in its simplest form:

```
<table>
  <tr>
    <td>data here</td>
  </tr>
</table>
```

- The `<table>` tags tell the browser there is a table being inserted.
- The `<tr>` tag says that there is a table row here.
- Lastly, the `<td>` tag tells the browser that there is a cell of tabular data.

To specify more rows or columns just add more `<tr>` and `<td>` tags. We'll see how to do this now.

Because basic HTML doesn't offer us complete control of where our images and text are placed, web designers employ tables like this to help control the layout. What we'll do is create a table and then add cells (dividing up the tables) to force the page to display in a certain way.

1. Select File > New. Dreamweaver will open a window that offers all kinds of pre-built pages and templates. Experiment with these later on when you feel a bit more comfortable with Dreamweaver. For now we're going to create a blank HTML page, so click on Basic Page and then choose HTML.

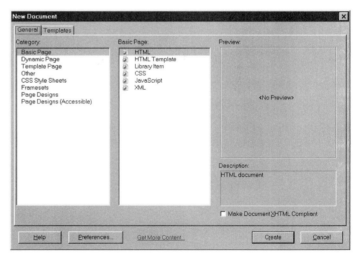

You'll now see a blank document. We're going to add a table to help control our layout. There are two ways of doing this and we'll look at them both here.

2. Click your mouse in the area you want to insert the table in the document window and then click on the Insert Table button in the toolbar.

3. You'll now enter the info for the table you're about to create. Enter 4 rows and 1 column. Make the width 775 pixels.

> *You could also set it to a percentage value. This would cause the table to resize automatically with the browser window. This is a good way to fill the browser with content no matter what size it's set to, but offers very limited layout control because the text and image would wrap wherever they wanted. This is not a method I recommend when piecing slices together. However, I will give you a tip on how to later on in the book.*

4. Set the Border to 0 because we want the table borders to be invisible, as discussed earlier. Also set the Padding and Spacing to 0 so that the images will line up against each other without gaps. The cell spacing sets the amount of space between adjacent cells in pixels. The cell padding sets the space between the cell contents and the cell borders.

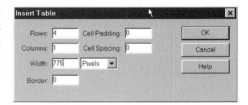

You'll see our basic table created:

5. If you look at the layout we are trying to create, you will notice that there are two columns in the main image window. Right click on the table cell we want to add the column to (that is, the bottom one) and choose Table > Split Cell.

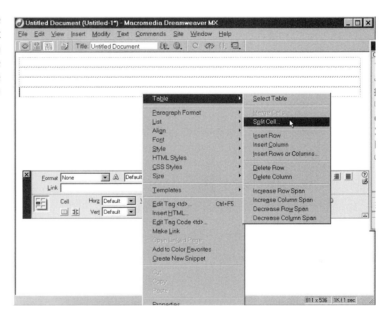

6. Choose 2 columns.

You'll now notice that the cell is split in two:

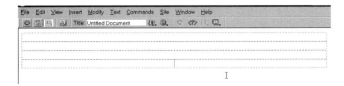

7. You can resize everything by simply clicking and dragging the cells.

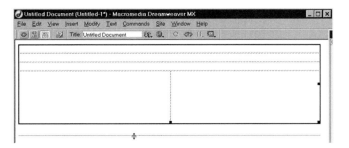

Now let's look at another way of creating the tables. This method was introduced in Dreamweaver 4.

Layout View

Layout View is a different way of looking at table layouts. The user creates a layout using visual boxes and Dreamweaver creates all the tables in the background. This is a more familiar method for designers migrating from the print world because of the familiar layout styles. Rather than defining table cells, you will just be dragging your mouse and creating boxes wherever you like on the page. You won't be exposed to the actual tables until you have switched back to Standard view.

1. Select File > New and create a blank document as we did before. Click Layout View at the bottom of the main Tools palette.

If you're using Dreamweaver's MX workspace, you can find this as shown below. Click on the Layout toolbar tab and then the Layout View button.

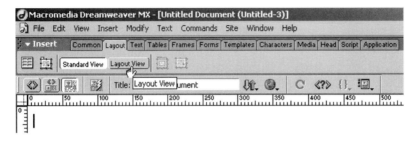

2. You'll see an instructional panel explaining how to use Layout View. Please read this and then click OK. You can also check the box if you don't want to see the message next time you switch to Layout View.

3. Click the Draw Layout Table button.

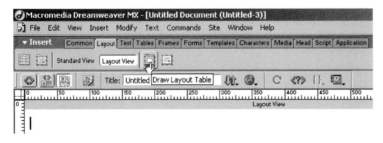

4. Now click and drag to apply the table to the page.

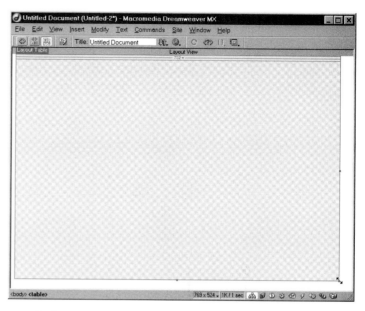

5. You'll notice how the width of the page is displayed at the top of the window. To get precise dimensions enter the width of 775 into the Property inspector. Don't worry about the height right now.

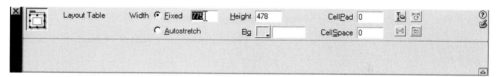

6. Take a look at our ImageReady page for a moment to discover the sizes for the cells we'll create. Click on the banner and notice the height in the inspector of 62. The width is not important since it's 775, the same as our page.

131

7. Let's create a cell that is 62 pixels high. Click the Layout Cell button right next to the Layout Table button and click and drag a cell in the top of our table.

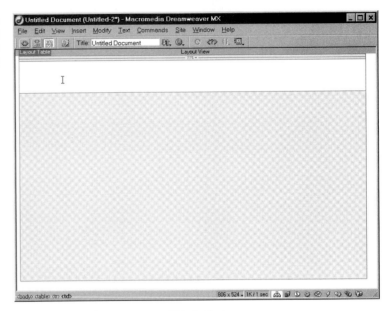

8. In the bottom of the window you'll see an HTML tag that says `<tr>`. This indicates that there's a table row. Click on it to select the row.

You'll now notice that the table cell is selected:

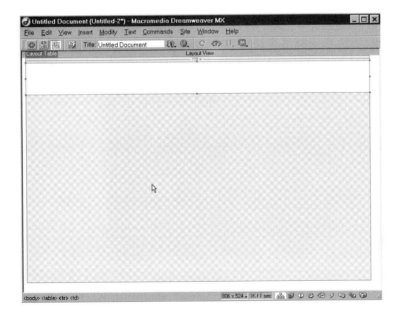

9. Enter a height of 62 pixels to resize our cell.

10. Go back to our ImageReady document and select the next image row. Click on the split view to see the image properties in a different way. You'll notice the height is 8.

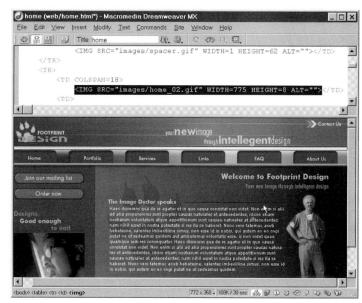

11. Draw another row in the same manner we created the previous one and set its height to 8 pixels.

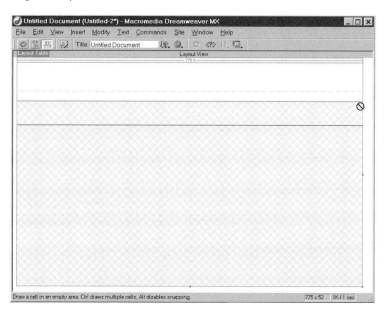

12. Continue until you have drawn all the cells.

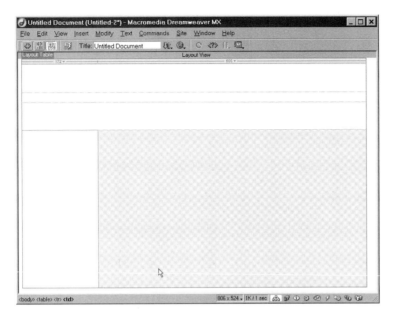

13. When you're finished, click on the Standard View button to return to the default layout.

You'll now see our table laid out. It's exactly the same as the table we built with the first method – we've just shown you two ways to reach the same result.

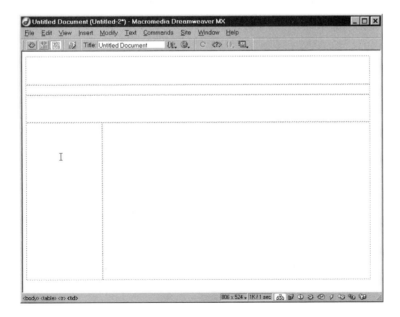

14. Save the page to the directory that you defined as your root.

Name it `index.html`. The index page is what the web browser looks for first when it reaches a web address.

You can use either `.html` *or* `.htm` *as the extension. Either will work just as well, but I recommend choosing one and sticking to it.*

You'll now see your new file displayed in the Site window of Dreamweaver.

Adding images

Now it's time to add pictures to the layout. We'll be loading our pictures into the table cells and they'll help to keep everything together. There are several ways to add images to the web page and we'll look at these methods now.

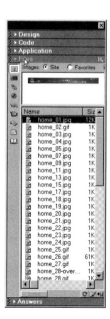

The first one is the Assets palette. This library will show all the assets. Assets are the images, Flash movies, custom colors and movies associated with the web page. When you add assets to the website they'll automatically be added to the Library.

1. To add them to the web page, just click and drag either the filename or the thumbnail. Drag them to your table cell.

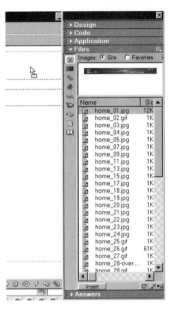

As soon as you release the mouse, the image will appear on your page.

2. Another way to add an image is to click in the cell where you want to insert the image and then click the Insert Image button on the toolbar.

The Select Image Source dialog will open.

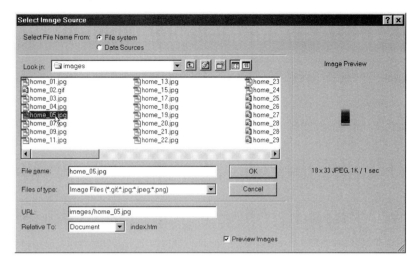

3. Navigate to your images directory and find your file. You can see a preview of your image to the right. Click OK when you're done and it will be loaded to your page.

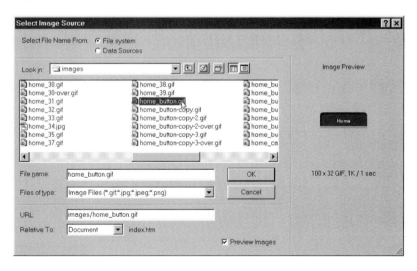

4. A third way of adding images is to drag them directly across from the site window into the document. You will see a small 'page' icon as you are dragging.

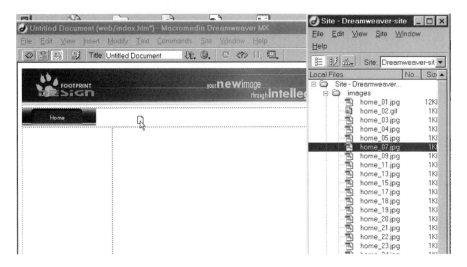

As you've already noticed, when you add smaller images into the horizontal table cell they will butt up against each other seamlessly. That's another reason why I've chosen a fixed width of 775 pixels. If we were using a percentage and the web browser was smaller than the working size, then the image would wrap and the layout would look terrible. Since we are using the set width of 775, the images won't wrap and the user will be forced to scroll horizontally to view the rest of the site.

5. You can also drag an image and place it between two existing images. While you're dragging take a note of where the mouse cursor is blinking.

6. When you release the button, the image will appear right where the pointer was.

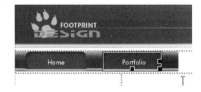

7. Add the rest of the images until the nav bar area is complete

Fixing the heights

Notice there's a gap on the row above the buttons. That's because the cell height is bigger than the image. Let's fix it.

1. Click on the image in the cell.

2. Just as we did before, click the `<td>` tag at the bottom of the window to select the table cell.

You'll see it selected:

3. Enter the height of the image. In this case it's 8 pixels.

Notice that the gap is now closed up and everything looks good.

Removing the page borders

We will now remove the blank space around the page so that the table lines up to the top and left of the page.

1. Open the Page Properties dialog. Modify > Page Properties or press CTRL/CMD+J

2. Enter 0 into all the margin fields. This will reduce the page margins to a value of 0.

Note, leaving them blank will not cause them to default to 0.

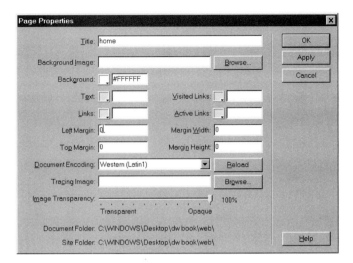

3. Click OK and the blank page margins are gone. This has the great effect of making our page design appear seamless with the browser.

Adding color to a table cell

Whenever possible, we should use Dreamweaver's color controls to color a cell. This is better than adding an image because the images would add to the overall file size, whereas adding a color command to a cell adds virtually nothing. This is a good reason to still use web-safe colors, because it makes it easy to match them.

1. Select the table cell we wish to color.

2. Click the Bg color swatch in the Properties panel. Choose a dark gray color by just clicking on it in the color palette that pops up. The palette contains web-safe colors.

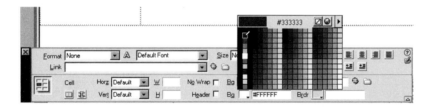

3. The cell is now colored.

Nested tables

We can also create **nested tables** in Dreamweaver. A nested table is a table within a table.

Using nested tables brings the advantages of more control over your layout and the ability to create more complex layouts. There are however disadvantages. Even though computers and browsers are becoming more advanced it's not recommended to use too many nested tables in a page if it can be avoided, as it may increase rendering time in older versions of browsers or on slower computers.

1. To add a nested table, place the cursor inside an existing cell and then add a new table. Choose the gray cell we just created; we are going to add some content in there. Click the Insert Table button in the toolbar.

2. Choose 6 rows and 1 column. Add 95% as the width. Because we're in a cell, the new table will span 95% of the width of the host cell.

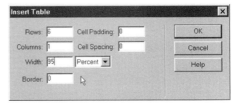

You will now see the new nested table.

3. Add an image to the table, using one of the three methods we explored earlier on.

4. Now add the two button images as well. They appear to blend in smoothly because their original background color is identical to the color we used to color the cell.

Aligning tables and content

1. Select the entire table. Click on the `<table>` tag at the bottom of the window in the status bar. The entire table is now selected.

2. Choose Center in the inspector and the whole table will be centered in the cell.

3. Now, to center the content of our nested table, click on the first cell and hold and drag your mouse through all the cells until they are all selected.

4. Click on the center alignment button and the content will be centered horizontally.

5. Click anywhere in the gray cell outside the nested table. Choose Top from the vertical alignment menu to position the table at the top of the page.

See how the page appears the same as the one we exported from ImageReady? Only this one will load faster because we are using HTML to display a lot of the page other than just images, which take longer to download. You really have to think about how to construct a page, and look for creative ways to cut down on the file sizes.

6. Let's finally add some color to the content area. Click inside it.

7. Choose a blue Bg color from the inspector.

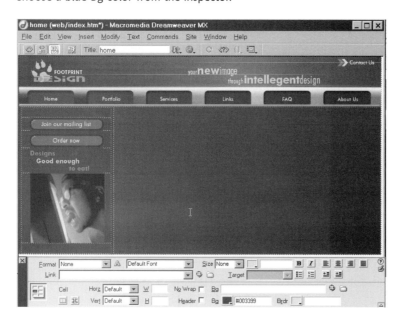

8. Preview the page in your web browser by pressing F12.

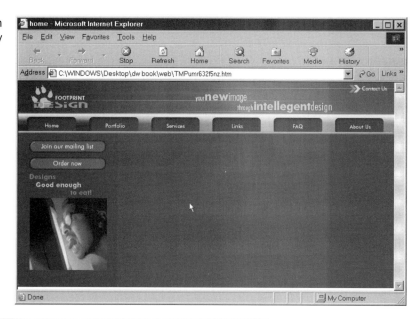

We could have begun with our ImageReady page, kept the original top area, deleted the content from the content area and used Dreamweaver to rebuild just this area. This is a method I employ a lot to quickly set up a site and save a lot of time. Don't be afraid to mix and match the technologies together. The aim is to use the software to help us design a functional site with the least amount of time and wasted effort and the smallest file size. Remember that there is always more than one way to do any task. You don't have to copy the methods shown in the book exactly. Adapt the techniques and use them to fit your workflow.

Summary and what's to come

We've really covered a lot of ground in a short space of time. We've successfully defined a root site and opened our ImageReady page in Dreamweaver. You've also learned about tables and explored different ways of creating and modifying them.

We've learned about inserting images into web pages and using tables to help in the layout. Finally we've learned a little bit about the cell properties and how to add color and align our tables.

In short, you've come a long way towards understanding how to use Photoshop, ImageReady and Dreamweaver together in a creative and practical way.

In the next chapter we'll be getting more in depth with Dreamweaver MX and looking at creating an entire site out of a single page. We'll learn about **Templates** and **Cascading Style Sheets**, as well as working with text and more.

5 Saving time with Dreamweaver

In this chapter...

We are now going to look at creating an entire site with several linked pages. We will explore such technologies as hyperlinks, templates and cascading style sheets to help slash the time it takes you to produce your pages and streamline your workflow. Over the course of this chapter we will explore:

- Hyperlinking our graphics and using image maps
- Templates in Dreamweaver
- Dreamweaver's site map feature
- Using cascading style sheets to visually enhance and co-ordinate our pages

Hyperlinking our graphics

A hyperlink is the method that HTML uses to direct the user to a different point in a web page or to an entirely different page altogether. It can also link to downloadable files or other images (say, in a thumbnail gallery). These links can be either text or images.

We are going to explore creating these links in Dreamweaver. On our project site we added the images for the buttons. They look complete but if you click on them they won't do anything yet (unless you use the exported page from ImageReady).

Creating links is very simple, but is made even easier in Dreamweaver.

1. Click on the first image, in this case the image we used as the Home button.

2. In the Properties panel look for Link. Type in the name for the link, or use the folder icon to open up a Browse... dialog box, so you can visually choose the file.

3. In this case we will link to the home page `index.html`.

Here you can also specify **Alt** (alternative) text. Originally, this was designed for people with non-visual browsers, or browsers where they had chosen to turn images off. This Alt text would give a description of what the image was. These days, they are useful for catering to blind or partially sighted visitors, but also good for generally giving extra information about an image or link.

That's it! The link is now active and whenever the user clicks on the Home button, they will be directed to the index.html page. The working page happens to be the index page, so if it were clicked on it would just reload this page. The reason we are putting the link in again is because soon this navigation will be on every page in the site.

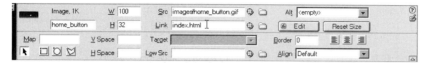

4. Add your links to all the buttons, naming each after the button title.

5. Do the same thing to the two buttons on the left nav.

All the buttons should now have links, except for the Contact Us button on the top-right. Up until now all the images have been the correct size for a button, but I'm sure you will have noticed that the Contact Us button is a part of a much bigger image. There is another method to get around this.

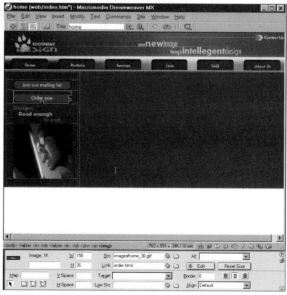

Image maps

We use an **image map** to define areas of an image which link to different places, meaning that your single large graphic can contain a number of links. Behind the scenes, an image map is simply an instruction to the browser which marks out certain areas as having certain properties. Using the tools in Dreamweaver we can define these clickable areas, which are also known as **hotspots**.

In Dreamweaver you will see three buttons on the lower left of the Property inspector. These are the drawing tools for image maps and you can use them to draw a rectangle, ellipse and polygon shape respectively

1. Click on the rectangular shape.

2. Now click and drag around the area you want to define as the image map.

When you release the mouse you will see the area filled with a semi-transparent color. Don't worry, this won't show on the actual web page; it is merely a visual guide for you while working in Dreamweaver.

3. Type the name of your hyperlink in the Link field. In this case we want the link to send an e-mail rather than open a new web page. Whenever you want to set up an e-mail link you must begin with 'mailto:' and then type the e-mail address you wish the e-mail to be sent to. For example mailto:webmaster@footprintd.com. When the user clicks on this link, their default e-mail editor will be launched with the defined e-mail address in the 'to' field.

If you also want to have the subject line filled in automatically, add ?subject="". So our e-mail link would look something like this: mailto:webmaster@footprintd.com?subject="message from web page"

4. Launch the page in your browser using F12 and test the links.

5. When you hold the mouse over a link, the target of the link is displayed in the browser's **status bar**, so you can see if it's pointing to the right page or not, or see if you've spelt the page's name correctly. If you click the links, you will get an error at this point because none of the linked pages exist yet (except of course for the mail link).

This is our next task.

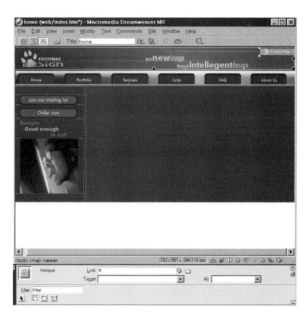

Introducing templates

Templates are an incredibly useful tool. A **template** contains all the parts of your website which are common to multiple pages, and means that when you change that basic template all the pages which use it are updated instantly.

For example, you could create a graphical navigation bar and then apply it to all the pages on the website. The beauty of this is that if you have to change something, you make the change once to the template and it's then applied throughout the entire site. The elements on a template are locked on the page so that changes are not made by accident. This is also useful when working in a team environment as you can control access to different page elements.

The process for creating a template is very simple, as you will see now.

1. Open the page you want to turn into a template. In this case we will use our sample page which is already opened. And do one of the following:

     Edit > Save as Template.

    Or choose Templates from the Tools palette and click the Make Template button.

2. Whichever method you choose you will now be faced with this dialog box:

This box will display all the current templates on this site. Since this is the first one we have created there is (no templates) displayed in the list.

3. Name our new template navigation and click Save.

The page is now saved as a template. If this template were attached to a page right now, you wouldn't be able to add any content or edit it at all. Because, by default the templates elements are all locked until we define them as editable. What we need to do is set a portion of the page as an editable region. This region is where all the content will be added.

Obviously, we are going to use the content table cell on our page.

4. Click inside the cell. Notice that the cursor is in the middle of the page. The alignment will also be applied to the content and any new content will be centered.

5. We really want the new content to begin at the top of the page. In the inspector choose Top under the vertical alignment drop-down.

> The vertical alignment setting is used to position items on a page. You can choose top, middle or bottom. This is similar to vertical justification on a page layout program. In a similar fashion, the horizontal alignment is used to position a page element either left, center or right. These are different to the text alignment, because they position items such as tables, images and blocks of paragraph text.

Notice that the cursor is now at the top of the section.

6. To make the table cell editable, click on the Define Editable Region button.

7. You will be asked to name the new region. Here I have called it 'content'.

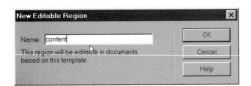

A box and a label will now appear on the new region. This indicates that we now have a new editable region.

I usually erase the sample text from the template as this will show up on the actual page. You may leave it if you wish, but I prefer not to. The pre-formatted text is useful if you are going to begin with a blank template page and add the content each time. It also acts as an indicator to show you where the editable region begins.

8. To delete it, select the text and press the DELETE key.

9. Press Save again and your template is now complete. We'll add this to our pages later on in this chapter.

As we begin to think about adding these other pages to our site, we'll need to consider how we're going to keep track of, and manage our pages, whether we have five or six or a hundred! Luckily, Dreamweaver has plenty of functions to help us with this, and we'll take a look at one of the most useful now.

Using a site map

A **site map** is a visual representation of the structure of your website. Dreamweaver can automatically create a site map for you, but note the site map created here is just within Dreamweaver and not actually a page you can upload to the Web.

> *If you really wanted a quick and easy site map page for your site, you could take a screen shot of the site map we're about to show, import it into a Dreamweaver page as an image and add hotspots to link each of the parts of the image to their respective pages.*

1. In the bottom of your screen, click on the Show Site launcher.

The site window will now open.

2. Click the arrow at the bottom to expand the view.

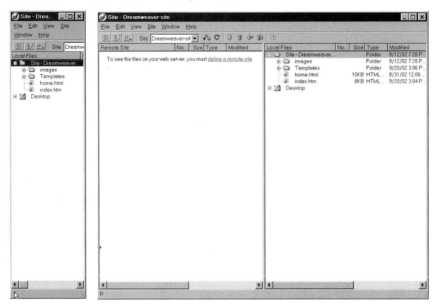

You will notice three buttons on the top left. The first is to show the files for the Remote Server (to be covered in **Chapter 7**) The second is for live data from the Testing Server. This is for testing databases interactively and is beyond the scope of this book, although friends of ED offer other books that cover this – see the back for details.

3. Click on the third button. This is the Site Map button. When the drop-down menu appears, choose **Map and Files**. Map Only would take the entire screen and hide the file browser.

Dreamweaver will now create a site map showing the hierarchy of your site.

All the sub-links are displayed in red and show a broken chain icon. This is because none of the files exist yet. They are shown because these are the links that we created on the index page, and Dreamweaver guesses that we intend to create them.

Let's create a sub-page and see how it affects the site map.

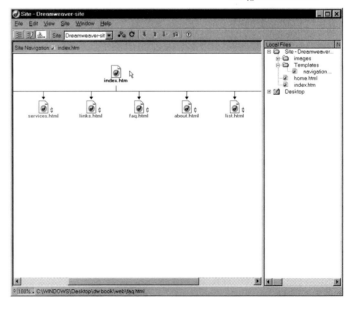

4. Create a new blank page.

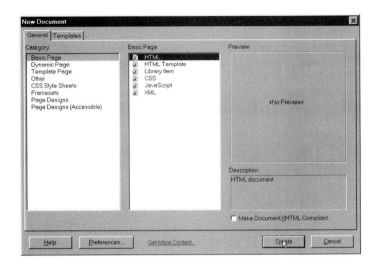

5. Save the page as `faq.html`.

6. Click Refresh in the Site window. This will update the display.

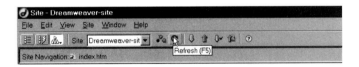

7. Now look at the site map and you will notice that the FAQ link is now in black and the broken chain is gone. This indicates that we have the two pages linked successfully.

> *The site map is an excellent resource and shows all the pages that we need to create at a glance.*

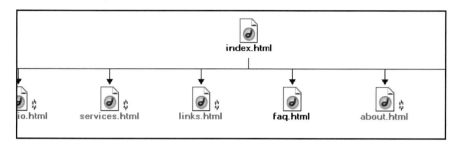

Now that we have created a sub-page, I will show you how easy it is to add the content and template.

Applying a template to a page

1. Open the `faq.html` page.

   We are now going to use a table to host the content. The reason we are doing this is to create some spacing and make the page look better than it would if all the content was jammed up against the edges.

2. Choose 1 row and 1 column for the table. Set it to 100% width so that it will span the entire content area. I have set a distance of 5 for the cell padding and spacing; this will provide our spacing for the content.

3. Begin to type your content into the table.

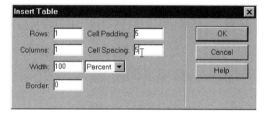

> *Whenever you press the* RETURN *key, a double line return will be added by default. In Dreamweaver the* RETURN *key will insert a <p> tag. The <p> is for a new paragraph. When you* SHIFT+RETURN *you add a <br> tag instead which gives you a single line break.*

Information about our company

We have been in business for 6 weeks and we are already #1 in our field. How is this possible? Apart from the fact that we started with a one billion dollar inheritance we offer some great services.

Low overheads

R

4. To add a single space press the SHIFT key at the same time as RETURN.

5. If you want to add a bulleted list, you can press the bullet button on the inspector.

You will now have formatted bullets on your page.

If you were to click the next button with the numbers, it would create a numbered list.

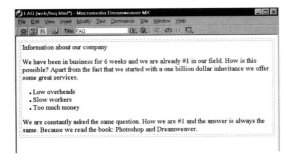

Now that our page is all formatted, let's apply our navigation to it.

1.   Choose Modify > Templates > Apply Template to Page.

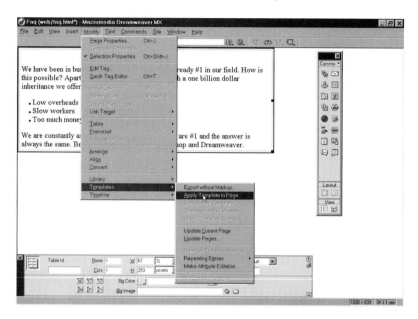

2.   You will be asked to choose a template from the list. This will be pretty easy in this case since we only have one! Choose navigation and click Select.

You will now see a dialog box asking you to map the definable regions.

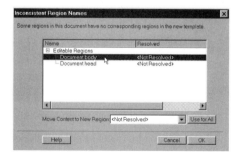

3. The document body is where all the existing page information will be placed on your page. Remember that we called our main definable region **content**? Choose it now from the list.

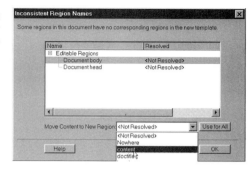

4. For Document head, choose head. This will now ensure that any header information will be moved to the right place on our HTML page. If no head field is shown, then proceed to the next step.

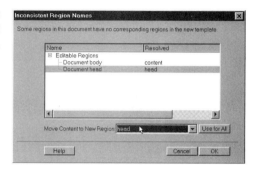

5. Click OK and the template is attached to the page with our formatted table in the content region.

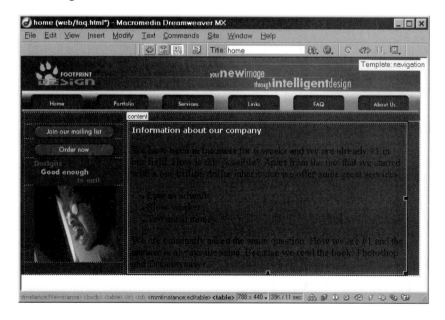

We are going to format the text using **style sheets**; this will save us from having to repeat ourselves over and over again.

Using Cascading Style Sheets

We can use CSS to save all the styles we use on a page and applying them site-wide. Not only can we format our text characters, we can also format link colors and behavior, background images and color and even the cursor's appearance.

Here is an example of a page on the web where CSS has been used to visually enhance a usually bland contact form:

Instead of applying the formatting information around the individual elements, we create a master CSS document. This document will reside on the web server with our site and the web pages will look to this for the formatting information.

Another advantage is that when you use CSS in a linked style sheet, you can make site wide style changes by modifying one file rather than having to change all of your pages. Much quicker and more efficient!

As you can see, with templates and easy style sheets, Dreamweaver offers us many time-saving features which help us to update our site quickly and with a minimum of effort.

Creating a new CSS document

1. Click on the CSS launcher.

2. The CSS style palette will now become active. Click the New CSS Style button.

3. The New CSS Style window will open and ask you for the name of the first style you want to create. We will format the main body text and call it body-txt.

4. Click OK.

Since this is the first style we are using and there is currently no master style sheet file, you will be prompted to create one.

5. Just enter the name with a `.css` extension and save it to the site root. I have called this `main.css`. This is the CSS document that the web page will look to for the formatting information.

6. Click Save.

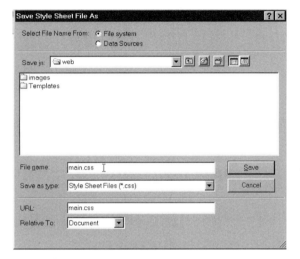

Now you will see the dialog box for the body-txt style. The title bar at the top says CSS Style Definition for .body-txt in main.css. This means the master file that will host all the individual styles will be called `main.css`. Note that the style name is always preceded by a period or full stop.

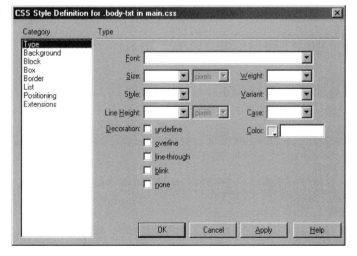

7. Choose the formatting options, including font, size, color, weight etc.

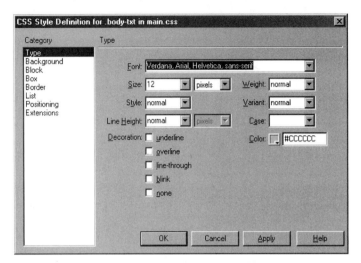

> We could devote the rest of this book to CSS if we broke down each and every option available to you. This is not the purpose of this book though. We just want to make you aware of the options and get you started creating CSS, but our focus is on designing web pages.

8. Click OK. Now let's add another style to our file.

9. Click the New CSS Style button in the CSS panel. Call this one heading.

> Note that you have an option for defining the style in `main.css` or this document only. If you choose `main.css`, the style will be added to the CSS file and be used in all the documents that are linked to the style sheet. If you choose this document only, then the style information will be embedded in this HTML page only. The purpose of this is if you want to format one page different than the rest, the local formatting will override all external style sheet information.

We are going to stick with the external style sheet since the method of creating is exactly the same.

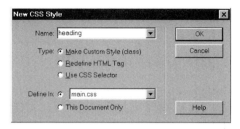

10. Define the style for the heading; I have made the character larger and bold.

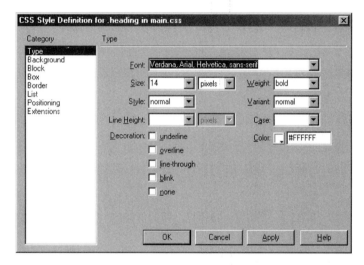

11. Looking in the CSS panel you will now see both our styles. You can continue and create as many as you wish.

Applying the styles

Now we have created our styles, it's time to put them to use. This is a lot easier than you may think. Select the area you want to apply the style to. When we click on the style, it will be applied to whatever region is selected at the time.

1. Select your the entire table, as you can see here.

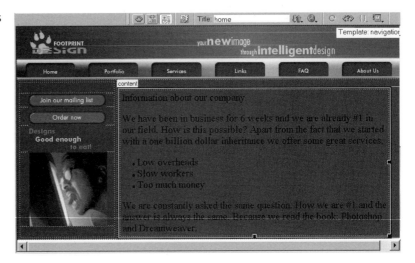

2. Click on the style you want to apply to the selection; in this case body-txt.

Wow! Our whole page was formatted in just one click! You can now see what a time saver it is to do a little preparation before building all our pages.

3. Highlight the heading with the mouse.

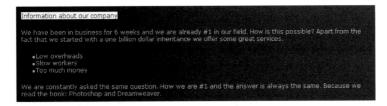

4. Click on heading in the CSS Styles palette.

5. The heading style is now applied to the page!

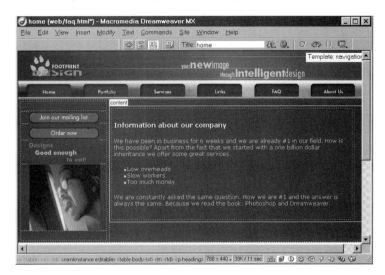

See how easy it is to apply styles to the page. We can reuse these styles as much as we want to and the benefits are threefold:

- We can now quickly format our web pages and the styles and formatting will be consistent throughout the site.

- We can update a single style sheet and the formatting and multiple pages will be automatically updated to reflect the change.

- There are more formatting options available to CSS than there are to plain HTML.

6. Press F12 to preview that page in your browser.

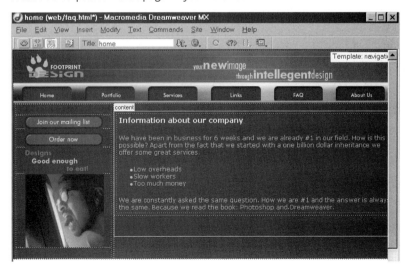

Here we have a perfectly formatted FAQ page using style sheets and templates. You can now create all the pages for your site and use the same formatting for each page.

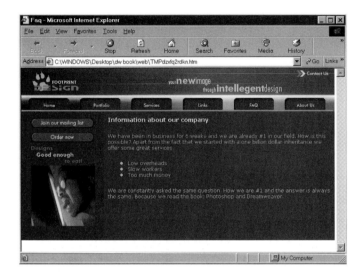

To edit your style sheets, just switch to the Edit Styles mode and double-click your style to bring the dialog back up.

Attaching an existing CSS to a document

We are going to apply the style sheet we created to a document. We can apply it to an HTML page or we can apply it to a template, the steps are exactly the same. The advantage of saving it to the template is that the CSS will automatically be available to all the pages that have the template attached.

Open our template document or any page you choose to attach the CSS to.

1. If you look in the CSS panel you will notice that there are no styles available.

2. Click the Attach Style button.

3. You will see the Link dialog open; click on Browse...

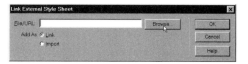

4. Find our `main.css` file and click OK.

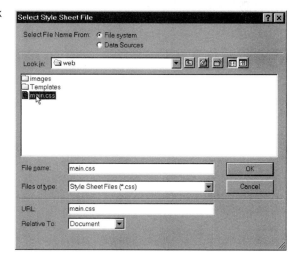

5. Check the Link radio button and then click OK.

The styles are now available to us.

6. Save the document.

If it's a template save as a template and you will see this dialog box:

7. Choose the pages to update like we did earlier on.

To update all just click Update without highlighting any pages.

All the pages that use the template will have the CSS available to them. Just apply the different CSS elements to different parts of the pages.

Now that we have the CSS attached to the template, let's create another new page; this time an About Us page. We will fly through this and you'll see how easy it is now.

This is another method of creating pages.

1. In the Site window click on the site root (the top level of our site).

2. Right-click (Command-click on Mac) and choose New File from the drop-down list.

 You will see a new document called untitled.htm.

3. Name it `about.html` and double-click to launch the new page.

4. Put the page title into the Title field. This is what will display in the title bar of the browser when the visitor views your page.

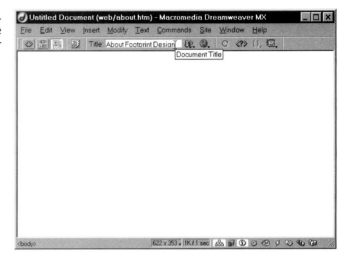

5. Add your blank table and enter your text.

> *We could have added the table to the template and we could skip this step. There are times, though, when you won't want the table on every page, like if you have an image that you want all the way to the edge. You could then choose to add the table to each page (only takes a few seconds) or create a second template. Multiple templates and style sheets are great for larger sites with a variety of layouts.*

6. Attach the template and format your page, just like we did earlier on using the CSS.

See how easy and quick it is to build pages now that we have the template and style sheet.

Adding a text link

Using what we've now learned, let's make the Contact Us text into a special text link.

1. Highlight the text with the mouse.

2. Just like we did for the image links, enter the URL into the Link field. We want this to be an e-mail address like in the Contact Us link. Type mailto:whoever@ youraddress.com.

The link is now active. The default color for a hyperlink is blue. The problem we now face is that the link is hard to read.

We could change the color of the link on the page by going to the Page Properties on the template. Instead, we are going to redefine an existing HTML tag (the linking tag) in our style sheet. This way we also have many more options than just changing the color.

3. Click the New Style button on the CSS Styles palette.

4. This time, instead of clicking Make Custom Style, choose the Redefine HTML Tag radio button.

5. In the top Tag drop-down, scroll for the tag a. <a> is the HTML tag for a hyperlink. Click OK.

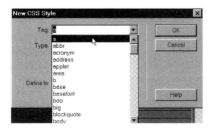

6. Now look at the Type section and choose another color. I used #FFCC66 which is a yellow/orange color.

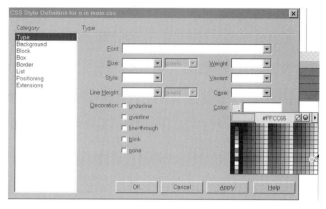

7. Click OK and all the text links will now be the new color instead of the default blue. This change will affect all pages with the style sheet attached.

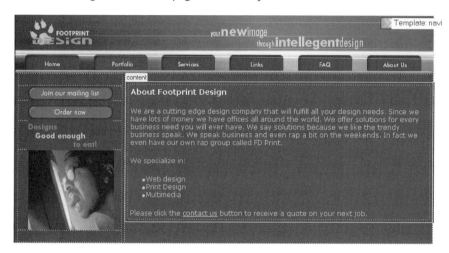

8. Preview in the web browser and check that the link now works and is displayed correctly.

Rollover effects on text links

We have re-colored our links text, but how about going a step further? By using CSS we can create rollover effects on all our text links. This is a lot of fun and a very fast way to add interactivity to your site.

This is achieved by using the **CSS selector**.

1. Click New CSS Style in the CSS Styles palette (note this will update every page using the same style sheet).

2. You will see the New CSS Style dialog box again. This time choose the third option – Use CSS Selector.

    Among other things, this option will give you the ability to change the way links respond to mouse behavior.

3. Click on the Selector drop-down and select a selector.

    There are several choices, all relating to links.

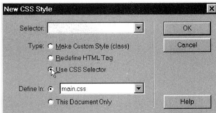

4. Choose the a:hover option. This will respond when the mouse 'hovers' over the link area.

5. Click OK and we will be taken to the Definition dialog. This is simple really. We are merely telling the style sheet what we want it to do to our link text when the mouse rolls over it.

    I chose the color white. This will cause the text to turn white when the mouse rolls over, indicating that we have a hyperlink just urging to be clicked.

> *In this dialog we can also change loads of other options, even the background color of links and the cursor that will appear when the mouse rolls over a link! You could also change the size of the text or make it bold or a number of combinations. I urge you to seriously consider the consequences of making the text bold or larger on rollover though. The downside of this is that the text can swell when the mouse rolls over a link, causing it to push the other text around the page and cause lines to rewrap. Very annoying for visitors.*

6. Press OK to apply

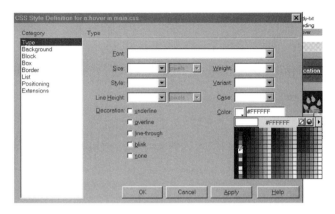

Open a page that has links and test them in your browser with F12.

Summary

You have now learned the art of quickly reproducing design elements and using them to easily build all the pages for a website. We have explored some advanced techniques such as templates and cascading style sheets. Feel free to build out the rest of your site using whatever content you desire.

In the next chapter we will look at creating rollover effects with images in Dreamweaver and we will also add some movement to our site using animated GIFs.

6 More advanced web techniques

In this chapter...

We'll move on to add additional interactivity and professional gloss to our website, concentrating on:

- Using Dreamweaver's Behaviors to add interactivity
- Updating images between Photoshop and Dreamweaver
- Web graphics and transparency
- Using animation and creating an animated rollover

In this chapter, we are going to tie everything together and explore some of the more advanced design features of Dreamweaver.

We have already produced rollover effects in ImageReady. Now we are going to explore two ways of creating them in Dreamweaver. Even though we can create them easily in ImageReady, it is invaluable to be able to create rollover effects in Dreamweaver so that we can implement and manage them in existing pages.

When we create a rollover in ImageReady, all the code is embedded into the HTML document that ImageReady produces. This means if we want to add a rollover to a pre-existing page, or change it later, we would have to re-export the HTML page and lose all our changes. With Dreamweaver we can insert rollovers into pre-existing pages and update them whenever we like.

Using behaviors

A behavior is a piece of JavaScript code that can be added in Dreamweaver without actually having to do any of the programming. At one point in time, the only way create a rollover effect was to actually write the JavaScript code that would swap to images on an 'event' (for example the mouse rolling over an area). the

We now have the **Swap Image** behavior that performs the same action, and it's so to use that anyone can do it. This is part of the reason there has been an explosion easy the use of rollovers on the web today. The other reason is that rollovers are the easiest way to make a page interactive and make the user experience more intuitive enjoyable. It's a good decision to make a button more tempting for the surfer to and click.

1. Open our template page, `navigation.dwt`.

When we make changes to our template, we update the entire site, so all effects we produce here will be updated in the rest of the pages, and this will the us having to repeat tasks. save

2. Select the slice that we want to assign the rollover to, in this case the button. Home

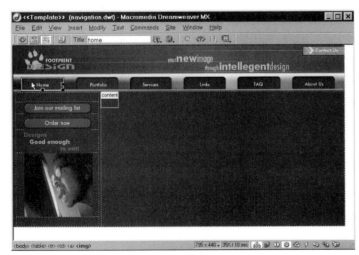

3. If it isn't already displayed, open the Behaviors palette of the Design panel by pressing SHIFT+F3.

4. Click on the [+] sign which is the add behavior button.

5. You will see a list of available behaviors. Choose Swap Image.

You will see the Swap Image dialog box. There are two main parts to this dialog box. The top pane (Images) is where you will choose the image that you want to affect with the rollover. The next option down, Set Source to:, is where you'll choose the image which will be replacing the original when the mouse interacts with it.

The selected image will be highlighted in the top part of the box. Our image is called home_button. This is the normal state, or the image that will be displayed when there is no mouse event detected by the browser.

You will see two checkboxes:

■ Preload images. This will cause the rollover images to be loaded into the browser's cache when the page loads, this will prevent a delay when the mouse rolls over the image.

■ Restore images on mouse out: if this box is not checked, the image will stay in the over state (changed images) even when the mouse moves away. Unless you are looking for a particular effect, always have this button checked.

6. To assign the rollover image, click the Browse button by the Set Source field.

7. Navigate to your images folder.

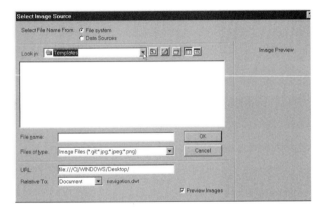

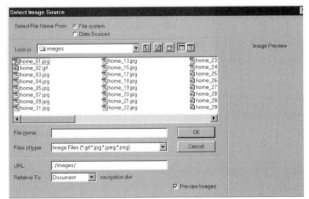

8. Find the over state of the image home_button; because we created the images in ImageReady, the over state of the button will be named the same as the original with the addition of the -over extension. The image we are looking for is home_button-over.gif.

You'll also notice a preview of the image on the right-hand side of the window. The preview will help you to locate the correct image.

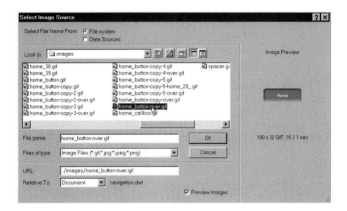

Your Swap Image dialog box should now look like this.

9. Press OK to continue.

You will see the behavior displayed in the Behaviors palette. Notice there is a Swap Image and a Swap Image Restore behavior.

*The left side of the palette will show the **Events** (when the user does something) and the **Actions** (how Dreamweaver will respond to the event).*

10. Press F12 to test in your browser, and check that the rollover works correctly. Repeat the steps to add the rollover effect to each of the buttons on your page.

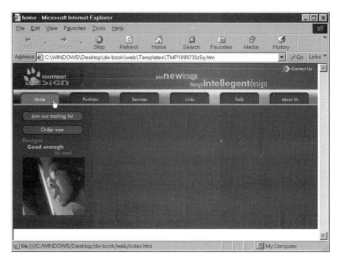

When you save the file you will see this dialog. This is because you are saving a template. Dreamweaver detects which pages are using the template and offers to update each page for you.

11. Choose each page on the list and choose either the Update or Don't Update button. Each page marked for updating will have the template changes applied to it.

> *By pressing the* Ctrl/Command *key and the* Shift *key, you can select more than one page at a time and mark them for updating or not to be updated.*

12. Press Update to apply the rollover effects to all the pages that are using the template.

You will be informed that the marked pages have been updated successfully.

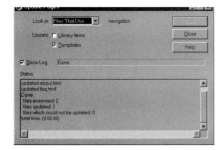

13. Open one of the pages that use the template and test that it is working correctly.

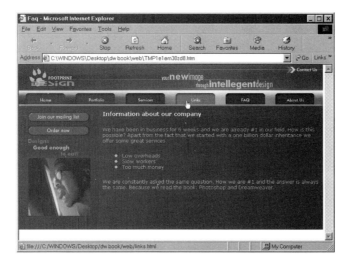

Another method of creating rollovers

There is another way to create rollovers in Dreamweaver, this will produce exactly the same result, except we'll be using one of the buttons on the toolbar. The method we just learned is the best way to add a rollover to an image already present on the page.

What if there is currently no image, but we want to add a new rollover image? In this case, the following technique is the best approach!.

1. Click the mouse into the area that you want to insert the new rollover image.

2. Click the Insert Rollover Image button.

3. You will now see this dialog box. You can name the image anything you want really, sometimes a more meaningful name can be easier to track later. You will need a name because the JavaScript written will use this name in the code it generates.

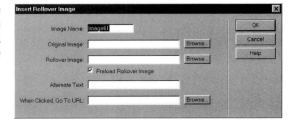

4. Click the Browse... button next to the original image field. We are going to insert the original static image. Find our normal state button. We will be inserting a mailing list button in this example. Of course you can choose any image you desire.

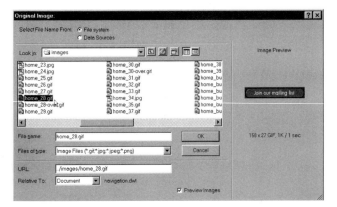

5. Click OK and click the Browse... button by the rollover image field. This is where we will assign the rollover image.

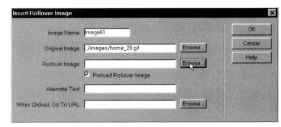

6. Find the over state (which must be created in Photoshop at an earlier time) and click OK.

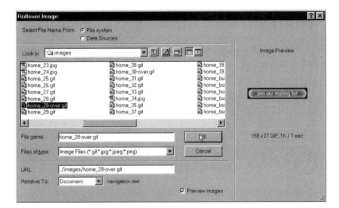

7. Finally enter the destination URL; this is where the button will take the user when they click on it.

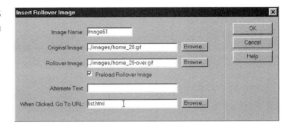

8. Press OK to apply the rollover image. Notice that the Behaviors palette shows the Swap Image action. The button on the toolbar is attached to the same behavior and is just another way to execute the same result.

Updating between Photoshop and Dreamweaver

We can change single slices in Photoshop and have them automatically updated in Dreamweaver, and this is one of the key elements of their interaction together.

I am sure you will have noticed that the word 'intelligent' is spelt wrong on the banner by now. Let's fix it.

1. Open the original page in Photoshop.

6

2. Using the Text tool, make the change to the word.

3. Now to export the new image and update our Dreamweaver page, File > Save for Web.

The Save for Web window will now open. This is a very powerful export window that allows us to optimize slices and more in Photoshop.

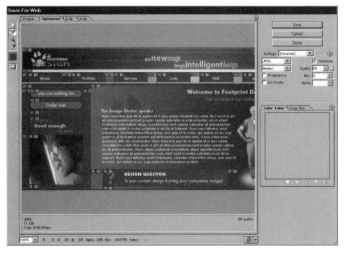

4. Choose the Slice Select tool for the left menu and click on the banner slice. For the optimization choose JPEG and 55. This is higher than I would normally use, but the slice has text and the logo on it, so it's very important that the quality is high here.

5. Click Save.

6. Navigate to our web folder.

Do not navigate all the way into the image folder. The Save for Web will produce its own image folder, or in this case direct the image to the images folder and overwrite the old banner image.

7. Under Save as type, we have the option to export images and an automatically generated HMTL page or Images Only. Choose Images Only. This will prevent a new HTML page from being generated and overwriting our existing page.

> *Ignore that fact that it says* .gif. *This is a confusing naming in Photoshop and the image will actually be saved as the type that was specified in the optimization settings (* .jpg *in this case).*

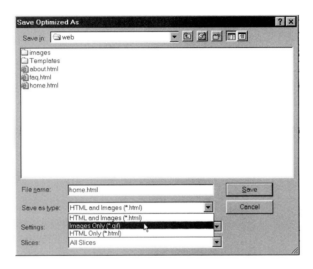

8. Under Slices choose Selected Slices. This will ensure that only the selected slice will be saved and Photoshop will ignore all the other slices.

9. When you have the settings correct press Save. Do not rename the file. It will be using the home.psd document, but Photoshop will generate a unique filename for the slice based on the slice name.

10. You will now have the option to replace the old banner with the new one we modified. If you see this dialog box, it is a good thing and means that we did everything correct. Click Replace.

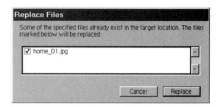

If you don't see the dialog box click Cancel, then check that our export path and names are correct!

11. Now open your Dreamweaver document and notice that the image has been replaced by the new one.

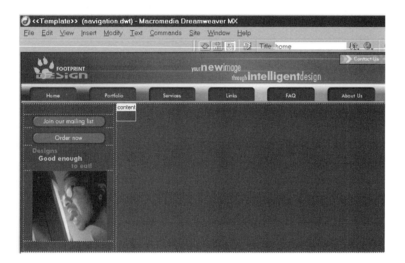

Using Transparency

A very popular and useful technique in web page design is using an image with a transparent background. This way we can cut the object from its background and place it against any colored background.

The first thing we will do is look at two methods of separating an object from its background in Photoshop. There are many ways of doing this, but we will just look at the two most popular.

Separating an object from its background

Method #1 – Magic Wand

Here is an image that we want to remove from its background so that we can use it on our web page. First we will look at the Magic Wand method; this works best for an object with a consistent colored background.

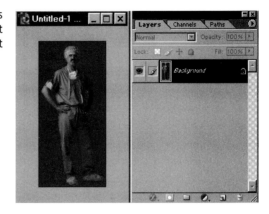

1. To begin with, take the flat image and convert it to a layer. If we keep it as a flat image, all we will do is replace the background with our current background color.

2. Double-click the background name in the Layers palette. You will see a New Layer box and a layer name Layer 0. Click OK and your background has now been converted to a layer.

3. Select the Magic Wand tool.

4. Using the Magic Wand, select all the blue area. You can adjust the tolerance of the wand if there is some slight variation in the background color.

5. Press the DELETE key and now you will see the image on a transparent background.

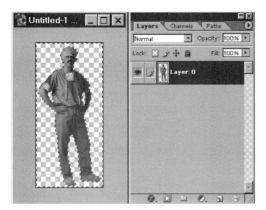

Method #2 - The Extract tool

This method is best for images with tricky backgrounds and soft edges such as hair on the images.

1. Start with our flattened image.

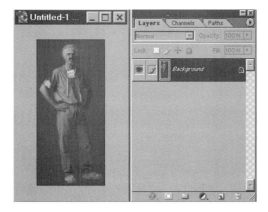

2. Select Filter > Extract from the main menu.

You will now see the Extract dialog box.

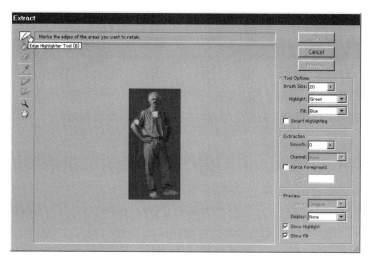

It works like this: Use the Highlighter tool to draw around the edges and then use the Fill tool to determine which part of the image you want to keep. Be very careful to make sure the edge highlighter is halfway between the image you want to keep and the background. Photoshop will then analyze the edge based on the colors, and decide which parts of the image to keep and which parts to discard. It's a little tricky at first, but the Extract tool is very powerful and will become a great ally to you once you have mastered its use.

3.   Choose the Edge Highlighter tool.

4.   Choose a small brush size. I have chosen a 7-pixel brush. Use a larger one for soft areas such as hair and fur or a smaller one for sharp clearly defined edges. You can use the [and the] keys to adjust the size of the brush while drawing. You can also press and hold the CMD\CTRL key to temporarily turn on the Edge Detect feature (Smart Highlighting). The Edge Detect will attempt to find the transition area and draw a very sharp line with the Edge Highlighter.

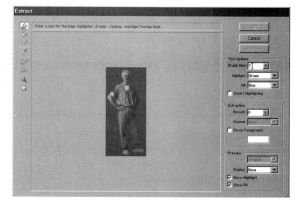

5. Draw around all the edges, being careful to keep half the selection inside the object and the other half outside.

6. Choose the Fill tool.

7. Click inside the object; this indicates which part of the image you want to keep.

8. Click Preview. If it looks right, press OK. Your image is now extracted from its background! Otherwise try making modifications using the Cleanup and Edge Touchup tools. Apply the extraction by clicking the OK key. If needed, any further modifications can be made using the Eraser and the History brush.

Creating a transparent image for the web

Whichever method you use to separate the image from its background is up to you. From here I will show you how to create a transparent image for the web.

> *There are two formats that support transparency: GIF 89a and PNG. PNG is a newer player on the field. The PNG format works well on modern browsers and will in fact support up to 256 levels of transparency whereas GIF only supports two. The disadvantage of the PNG format is that it often produces a large file size and that it is not supported on older browsers. For this example I will be using GIF. The process for PNG is identical.*

1. With the extracted image on a layer and the background hidden, click File > Save for Web.

2. The Save for Web dialog box will open.

3. Make sure that the Transparency box is selected and choose 256 colors for this case. If you are using an image that uses fewer colors, choose a more reduced color palette – this will save file size.

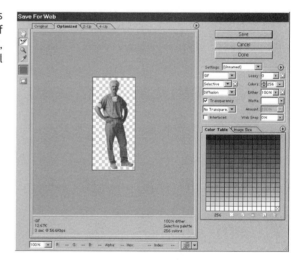

> *The next option is called Matte. If you choose none, the image will remain in its current transparent state, but could produce jagged edges. The matte will actually pad the edges with a color of your choice and produce nice sharp edges on the background when a corresponding color is chosen for the matte. Be sure to save a copy of the PSD in case you want to change the background color later and then need to re-export the image with a different colored matte.*

4. For this example we will be placing it on our web page with a blue background, so choose Other.

5. Enter the hexadecimal number for the same blue as used on the background color of the example page or choose it visually from the color picker.

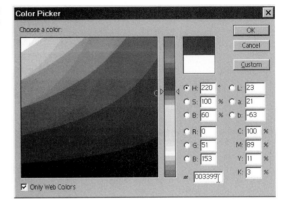

Notice that the edges are now surrounded by a thin strip of blue.

6. Save our image into our images folder as a GIF. I called it `doctor.gif`.

You can now close Photoshop if you wish.

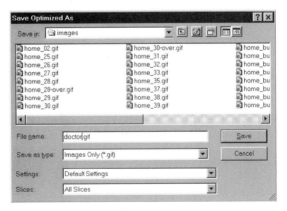

7. Open your web page in Dreamweaver. See how I've used tables to rebuild the content area of the home page with text rather than images. You have already learned how to do this earlier on in the book.

8. Place the insertion point in the text box. This is where our image is going to be placed.

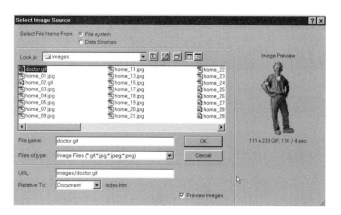

9. Click the Insert Image button from the toolbar, and browse to `doctor.gif`.

This image will now be inserted in the page, but it has made the text go crazy because as a default the text will not wrap around images.

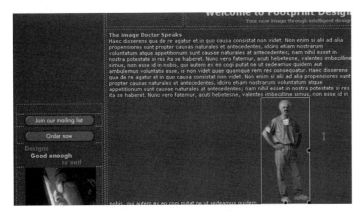

10. By choosing the Align options for the image we can make the text wrap around the image borders. Let's choose right-aligned.

You will now see the image right-aligned and a little alert symbol in the page showing that a right-aligned image is inserted at that point.

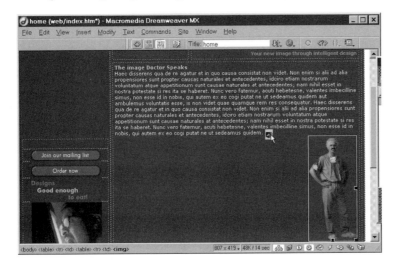

11. Click and drag the alert symbol to the beginning of the paragraph of text. Notice that the image will move up with it and the text will now wrap correctly.

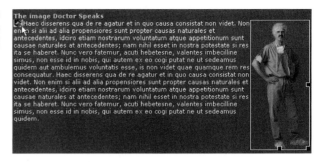

Here is our page with the transparent image inserted. The entire page with images is still only 51K!

12. Press F12 to preview in the web browser. Are you beginning to see how well Photoshop and Dreamweaver work together? It's no wonder that they are the most popular programs for web designers!

Animation

Animated GIFs are a great way to add movement to a web page. Be warned though, that too much movement and animation can be very distracting to a design and increase the file size. The best way to do it is to have short animations with intervals of non-movement. This gets your point across without frustrating the viewer.

We'll add an animated banner to the top of our Links page.

1. Launch ImageReady and choose a new document; make it 500x35 pixels.

2. Choose the foreground color, use the same color as we used for our background color on the example site – #003399.

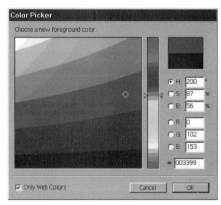

3. Fill the image with the color. This will give us a seamless background for our animation.

> *We could have produced a transparent image like we did earlier on in the chapter, but I have found that a transparent animated GIF can have a fairly heavy file size, so a fixed color is good when you can get away with it.*

4. Choose the Text tool.

5. Type in the word Links and format it. Make the color white and the size 24, and use a clean readable font like Arial.

6. Now open the Animation palette; by default, it is nested with the Slice palette. You will see a number one on the corner, this means that we currently have an animation consisting of one frame. It doesn't take a rocket scientist to figure out that a 1-frame animation is actually a static image.

7. Frame 1 will be the starting point for our animation. Click the New Frame button.

8. We now have two frames. ImageReady actually produces the effect of animation by quickly switching out the image on each frame in quick succession and thus producing the effect of movement, much like the frames on a movie.

9. With the second frame selected, drag the text to the right side of the window.

We now have a two-frame animation of the text moving from the left to the right of the window. It is very jerky and fast because there are only two frames. We need to add some more frames in between the two in order to smooth the animation.

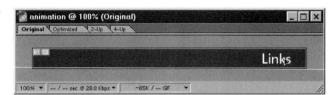

ImageReady has a feature that will automatically create these in-between frames. This process is called "tweening". The term is borrowed from movie animations. There would be a lead artist who would create all the pivotal animation slides. A young apprentice would spend all his/her time producing the 'in-between' slides, hence the apprentice was actually called a "tweener."

10. Click on the arrow at the top right of the Animation palette. When the drop-down menu appears, choose Tween.

The Tween dialog box will now appear.

11. First we have the option to tween with the previous or next frame. We will choose previous because we want the new frames to appear between frames 1 and 2.

12. The next option lets us choose the amount of frames we want to add. Five is usually more than sufficient.

> *Remember that the more frames we add, the larger the file size will be.*

13. We can select either the selected layer or all layers. This will cause the tween function to look to all layers or just the selected layer for changes.

The next three options are:

- Position: This will create a motion animation where only the position will change.
- Opacity: You can use this option to fade objects in and out.
- Effects: This is good for fading in layer style effects.

> *You can choose one of these effects or combinations of all the effects if you wish. We are just going to create a simple animation in this example so that you will understand how the animation features work. I suggest that you spend some time experimenting with animations on your own.*

14. When we click OK, ImageReady will create the five frames for us and we will now have a seven-frame animation.

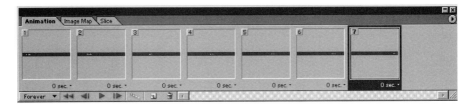

15. The default delay time is set to 0. This means that the animation will play as quickly and smoothly as it can. To add a delay time to any of the frames select the arrow next to 0 sec and choose a delay time. This will cause the animation to pause on the selected frame for the set amount of time. I choose 10 seconds for the last frame. This will cause the animation to pause for 10 seconds before looping to the beginning again. By default the animation will always loop, or repeat itself.

16. By clicking on the arrow by Forever you can set the looping preferences. Choose Once for no looping or choose Other for a custom amount.

17. Enter 5 to have the animation repeat five times and then stop.

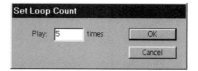

18. Click the Play button to preview the animation.

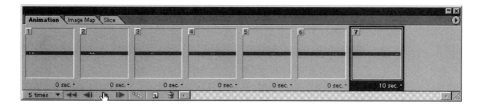

19. Press the Stop button to stop the preview.

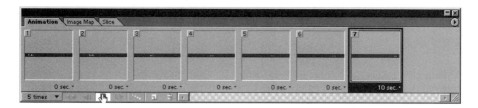

20. You could also click the Preview in Browser button to see what the animation will look like in a web browser. I recommend this option as the animation is usually faster and smoother in a web browser that it is in ImageReady.

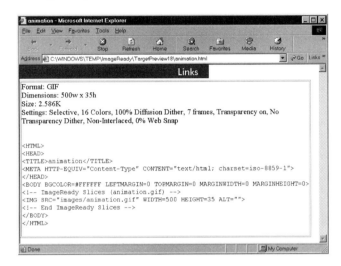

21. We can also optimize the animation just like we would any image. Choose GIF as the option, since a GIF is the only graphics format that will support animation.

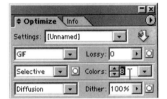

When you are satisfied with your animation save it, File > Save Optimized As..., name it and put it to your image folder.

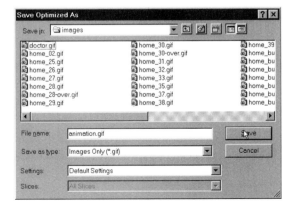

22. Now place the image into Dreamweaver and align it to suit your tastes.

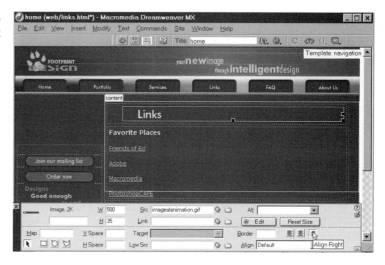

23. Press F12 to preview in your web browser. It looks like the animation is working perfectly.

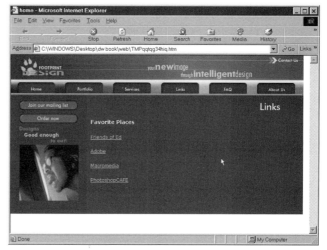

Animations are great for use in web-banners and logos, but what if we want to combine them with our other new interactivity technique, the rollover effect?. I'll now show you how to created a fully animated rollover!

This tutorial was originally featured in a chapter I wrote for friends of ED's Photoshop Most Wanted: Effects and Design Tips. It's a subject I am often asked about.

Creating an Animated Rollover

Here we'll incorporate what you've just learned, but with the additional attraction of an animation. When your mouse rolls over the button, the button will light up and the doors will slide open. We are going to create the slices and rollovers in ImageReady. Then we are going to create an animation, also in ImageReady. Lastly, I will show you a work around, to switch the static rollover image for a cool animated one.

> *Because this tutorial is more specific than some previous ones, you'll probably want to follow using my source file. You can download it from the Files link on the Photoshop & Dreamweaver book page at www.friendsofed.com. It's called* `animated_rollover_before.psd`. *The finished rollover is also supplied for you to play with later.*

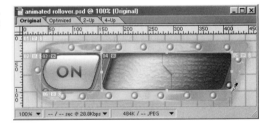

1. Using the Slice tool, make a slice around the button.

2. Make a second slice around the door area. Notice that all the other slices are automatically generated.

3. Using the Slice Select tool, choose the ON button that should be slice 03.

4. In the Slice palette, assign a link under URL.

5. Let's create the rollover. Switch to the Rollovers palette and click on the Create Rollover State button. The Over state is now added.

6. Show the button lit layer; this will give the impression of the button glowing.

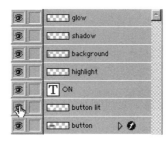

Here's the result:

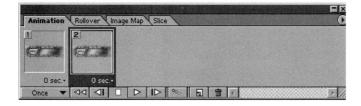

On the Layers palette, there are two layers called door right and door left. These are the doors that we will animate soon.

7. Open the Animation palette. Click on the duplicate frame button to add a new frame.

8. With the new frame selected (frame 2), select the door left layer.

> *Important: at this point, make sure you change to the Move tool on the toolbar or your slices will move instead of your layers.*

9. Using the arrow keys on your keyboard, tap the left key until the door is slid all the way to the left. Hold the SHIFT key to nudge the image in increments of 10 pixels instead of 1 pixel to save time.

10. Select the door right layer.

11. Use the right arrow key and move the door all the way to the right. We now have the ending frame of the doors open.

Looking in the Animation palette, you will see two frames. Frame 1 is the image with the doors fully closed, whilst Frame 2 is the image with the doors fully open.

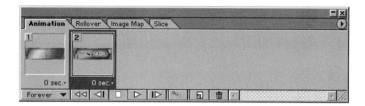

12. For a smooth animation, we will need to create some in-between frames of the doors opening. We learned how to do this in the last tutorial, so click the little arrow in the top right of the Animation palette and choose Tween.

13. You will see this window pop up. Choose 4 for the number of frames to add. Leave all the other settings as default, and click OK.

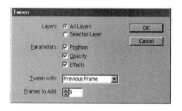

The four frames are now generated automatically. We now have a total of six frames for a very smooth animation.

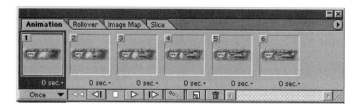

14. Press the Play button to test the animation. Press Stop when you are done.

As mentioned earlier, these animations loop by default. In a lot of cases this is good, but not here. We want the doors to open once and then remain open. If your animation is looping, go to the button in the bottom left and change the looping from Forever to Once.

15. Click the Play button to test the animation again. The doors should slide open and then stay open.

Optimizing the slices

Now that the animation is working, it's time to output the page.

1. Choose a JPEG for all the slices except for the door slice (04).

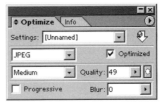

2. Select slice 04 (the doors).

3. In the Optimize palette, change this slice to a GIF. We made it a GIF because only GIFs can be animated.

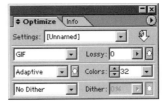

4. We will now output the document just like we did in the last tutorial so select **File > Save Optimized As**.

5. Create a new folder and export the new page to that location. Save as type: HTML and Images should be selected as well as All Slices. Click Save to generate the code and sliced images.

6. We are now ready to launch our new animated remote rollover. Go to your saved folder and find the animated-rollover HTML document. Launch it in your favorite web browser to view.

As your mouse goes over the button, the button glows and the doors slide open. I'm sure your brain is thinking of lots of uses for this trick now. You can really spice up your web pages with animated rollovers and stand out from the crowd.

Summary

We have now finished fleshing out our web site. You have learned how to create an entire site using templates, style sheets and site maps. We have also learned how to add tables, images, rollovers and animations to our websites.

Of course, I've just given you the bare information with which you can create great visual websites of your own, with your own creative combination of stunning Photoshop graphics, neat and clever ImageReady slicing and some cool animations, all wrapped up in a web-ready Dreamweaver package.

The next step is taking all this to the web itself, and in the next and final chapter we will discuss your options and get your site live on the Internet!

7 Getting your site online

In this chapter...

It's time to put your site on the Internet, and we have all the tips you need to make the most from your hosting company. We'll cover:

- Domain names and how they work
- Registering a domain name and using web forwarding
- Hosting your site – all the options explored
- Uploading your site using Dreamweaver
- Matching and synchronizing your files

Now you have built your website, the links are working, the pictures are pretty and the information is sizzling. There's only one problem. You're the only person who can see your work of art! In this chapter, we're going to discuss what is involved in getting your site live on the web for the whole world to see.

Your website currently resides on your hard drive; in order for it to be accessible by the whole world, you will need to transfer the files to a **web server**. A web server is another computer somewhere that is hooked up to the Internet with a constant, super-fast connection. It is all these computers linked together that make up the World Wide Web.

In the simplest terms, you'll need two things – a **domain name** and **web space**. These can be provided by the same company or different companies. The domain name is the URL of your site, and you need to set this up so that when people type this in, your domain host directs them to your site.

The web space you'll need is the actual physical place where you'll store your site files. This will be on an actual computer somewhere, as outlined above. Usually bundled with this service are other features such as e-mail.

> *Note, you can own a domain without taking any web space. If you want to grab your favorite name before someone else does, you can register it and host your site later. We'll look at both these in turn.*

Domain name

The **domain name** is what people will type into their browser to bring up your site, e.g. www.footprintd.com or www.friendsofed.com. The name is up to you and you can also choose from a range of country-based extensions.

The most common extensions (domains), originally for the US but generally recognized worldwide, are:

- .com   Company
- .net   Internet service
- .org   Non-Profit organization
- .gov   Government Department
- .edu   Educational Institution

There are also many others including country specific ones such as .co.uk for the United Kingdom and .ca for Canada.

Choose a name that is short (people don't like to type), is memorable, and is identifiable with your website. One of the problems you will face today is that a lot of the good names are already taken, so you may have to be creative in selecting your name.

Your domain can include any letters or numbers, and also the dash symbol (although it cannot start or end with the dash). No other symbols are allowed. It can be between 2 and 67 characters long (including the .com) but the shorter the better.

To select a name you will have to go to a domain wholesaler site. The exact process may be different for your country you are living in, but the principle will still be the same. In the last couple of years, the government deregulated the industry, and there are now many discount vendors on the web, meaning you can get domains for as little as $5-$10.

Shop around for the best price and features. We'll take a walk through an example in just a few paragraphs' time.

Web forwarding

With web forwarding, which comes in a few guises, you can own a domain (or a number of domains) and have them point to web space elsewhere. For example, you might set up a domain and web space at www.footprintd.com, but additionally you might want www.footprint.co.uk and www.footprint.ca as well. You do not need to have three independent sites, just the capacity to forward people who type in your domain to the space you designate.

More often, you might use web forwarding to forward users to free web space provided by your ISP. This is becoming a common feature that ISPs offer, and buying a domain and forwarding it invisibly to your free space can be a very affordable way of managing a professional-looking personal site.

Web forwarding takes two main forms: **redirection** and **cloaking**. Redirection means that people entering www.footprintd.com will have their browser instantly sent to another address. Cloaking is when your 'other' address is concealed within an HTML frameset. Without going into the details, this means that your domain name www.footprintd.com would remain in the browser address bar, making the web forwarding practically invisible. This has the advantage of appearing much more professional.

Registering your name

Finding a registrar can be a tricky process, there are so many to choose from. Keep in mind the services you need now (like e-mail addresses and web-forwarding), and also the services you might need in the future to make your choice one which will serve you in the long term.

*Be aware that moving your registration from one company to another can be a costly and time-consuming business. If you come to need services which your registrant cannot offer, you may have to move and it can be very awkward. This is why future-proofing is important. You might also want to check to see if your chosen registrant charges for domain transfers, but note that they may have a different policy for transferring **to** them than for from them transferring **away**.*

To be honest, word of mouth is arguably the best way to find a good domain/site host. If you know anyone who has a site, ask them what features they got, and more importantly, about the level of service. Make sure it's right for you, and don't always trust the flashiest banner or the cheapest advertised price. There can sometimes be hidden costs.

Let's take a walk through a typical process. We'll use as an example Xcalibre.co.uk – the internet company which hosts friends of ED's popular Flash community at www.phpforflash.com.

Begin with a search to see if your name is available.

Some sites will allow you to choose an extension at this stage, but in this age of Internet saturation, most hosts will instead show you all possible combinations and mark them as available or taken.

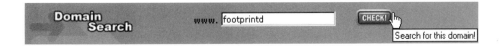

You've probably figured out by now that our choice to go with www.footprintd.com was because footprintdesign was already taken! As you can see, we have no competition here and can register as many variations as we wish.

Search Results

Please note the new rules for registering me.uk domains

Domain	Status	Cost	Length	
footprintd.me.uk	Available	£9.95	2 Years	Add to Order ☐
footprintd.biz	Available	£17.50	2 Years	Add to Order ☐
footprintd.info	Available	£17.50	2 Years	Add to Order ☐
footprintd.co.uk	Available	£9.95	2 Years	Add to Order ☐
footprintd.org.uk	Available	£9.95	2 Years	Add to Order ☐
footprintd.com	Available	£19.95	2 Years	Add to Order ☐
footprintd.net	Available	£19.95	2 Years	Add to Order ☐
footprintd.org	Available	£19.95	2 Years	Add to Order ☐
footprintd.uk.com	Available	£55.00	2 Years	Add to Order ☐
footprintd.ltd.uk	Available	£9.95	2 Years	Add to Order ☐
footprintd.plc.uk	Available	£9.95	2 Years	Add to Order ☐
footprintd.us.com	Available	£55.00	2 Years	Add to Order ☐
footprintd.eu.com	Available	£55.00	2 Years	Add to Order ☐
footprintd.br.com	Available	£55.00	2 Years	Add to Order ☐
footprintd.uk.net	Available	£55.00	2 Years	Add to Order ☐
footprintd.gb.com	Available	£55.00	2 Years	Add to Order ☐
footprintd.gb.net	Available	£55.00	2 Years	Add to Order ☐
footprintd.de.com	Available	£55.00	2 Years	Add to Order ☐
footprintd.ru.com	Available	£55.00	2 Years	Add to Order ☐
footprintd.cn.com	Available	£55.00	2 Years	Add to Order ☐
footprintd.qc.com	Available	£55.00	2 Years	Add to Order ☐
footprintd.no.com	Available	£55.00	2 Years	Add to Order ☐

Next Step!

footprintd.com   Available   £19.95   2 Years   Add to Order ☑

You will possibly be asked if you want to add **web hosting** to your offer. This is where our explanation of web space earlier comes in.

Web hosting

A web hosting account is what you will upload your files to. Your web host is the operator of the computer (the server) that will store your website and make it available over the Internet to anyone anywhere in the world.

As mentioned earlier, you might want to limit yourself to a domain and use free space elsewhere for the time being, but for the sake of the tutorial, let's assume you want to host your site with your domain registrars. There will be a multitude of options presented to you whatever you choose. Here is a rundown of the most important ones:

:: **Hosting Standard**

:: Service	Hosting Standard	Hosting StandardPlus
Websites	1	1
Web Space	50MB	50MB
POP3	5	10
Aliases	✓	✓
Control Panel	✓	✓
Email Forwarding	✓	✓
Full FTP	✓	✓
PHP	✓	✓
SSH	✓	✓
Free Domain Transfers	✓	✓
Access Raw Log Files	✓	✓
Bandwidth	1.0GB/month	2.0GB/month
Dedicated CGI Bin	✓	✓
Preinstalled CGI Scripts	✗	✓
Email Support	✓	✓
Telephone Support	Premium Rate	National Rate
Auto Responders	✓	✓
Web Statistics	normal	enhanced
MYSQL Database	£10.00	✓
WAP Support	✓	✓

How much web space?

This is how much hard drive space they will give you on their server for you to store your files. Most hosts will offer you way more than you will actually need.

Remember that although your PSDs may be several MB in size, your site has been designed and optimized to be as small and quick to download as possible. This means your final site shouldn't take up very much space at all, but it's always good to have a comfortable amount of extra space for expansion.

> *Note that this amount is only the physical space you take up on their server, and **not** anything to do with the number of visitors you are allowed.*

How much bandwidth?

Bandwidth is a crucial term in web circles. Bandwidth is the amount of **transfer** you are allowed on your account.

Think of it as like when you are downloading a file. If you have a dial-up modem, you can only download so much at a time. You might have several downloads at once, but if one download was taking up all your bandwidth, you'd start finding it difficult to surf at all! Of course, your host has a very high-speed connection. Your bandwidth limit simply expresses how much of that connection you are allowed to use up, and is specified by an amount of transfer in MB.

This is another good reason for keeping your files small. If you have a huge homepage with unoptimized graphics and multimedia, and it weighs in at 500K, then if your bandwidth limit is 1GB per month (just over 1,000MB), after 2,000 visits your site will stop functioning or, more likely, your host will charge you for the excess.

On the other hand, if your site is just 50K, then you can have 20,000 visitors!

Bandwidth requirements are completely dependent on file size and traffic. If you have large pages and many visitors, you might need more, but you are unlikely to need more than a standard 1GB per month for the time being.

> *Check with your prospective host to ask what their charges are if you exceed their limit, and how easy it will be to upgrade to a higher bandwidth account if you need to.*

E-mail

Well, this is pretty essential. You're going to want yourname@footprintd.com and possibly more e-mail addresses. There are a few options available:

- POP3 – standing for Point-of-Presence, this is a standard e-mail system whereby your mails are stored on your server, until you come online and download them using Outlook, Outlook Express, Netscape Messenger or the like. You can send mails also by creating them in your client and connecting to the web to send.

- E-mail forwarding – this is where mails to yourname@footprintd.com are forwarded to an existing mail address, e.g. yourname@hotmail.com. Note that you cannot send mails which will appear as being from yourname@footprintd.com under this set-up.

Assess what your needs are. If this is for a client, then you will need to ask them how many distinct addresses are required and what type. Mark up whatever addresses you can think of, e.g. sales@footprintd.com, info@footprintd.com, etc, and work it out from there.

Support

You're always going to need some kind of support, even if it's just to report technical problems. Most hosts will offer some kind of support, but beware of premium-rate numbers, which mean you pay out just to report problems.

Good e-mail support with reasonably fast responses can be every bit as good as telephone support. Again, assess what you need and make sure you don't overlook this important service.

Dynamic capability

We have just created a **static** site, but sites which feature login forms, contact pages, forums and mailing lists require additional technology on the part of the host.

You'll probably have heard of ASP, PHP or ColdFusion. These languages allow your server to interact with your users and with a database, meaning you can store user information and control the pages they see, depending on the information they give. You might want to add this kind of functionality in the future, and the good news is Dreamweaver MX has all the tools, although that's a book in itself.

> *It is indeed a book in itself, and friends of ED have published Foundation Dreamweaver MX to cover this. You might find the first few chapters cover some of the same ground as this book, but the rest of the book covers advanced Dreamweaver MX techniques, as well as connecting to a database and creating more user-interactive pages using PHP.*

Often you pay for such capabilities, so again it is useful to ask how easily it can be 'bolted on' if you need it in the future. PHP, being an open source (free) language is often provided without charge, and it is one of the most respected and robust server languages available.

Control Panel

Most web hosts will provide you with some kind of control panel, through which you will administer certain areas of your site, and also change e-mail information or passwords. A good control panel makes it extremely easy to manage your site and make updates.

Your control panel might also allow you to upload your files. Otherwise, you should ensure you get FTP access in order to do this directly. A typical FTP (File Transfer Protocol) address would be ftp.footprintd.com, and you can use Dreamweaver to upload your files, as we'll see in a few moments.

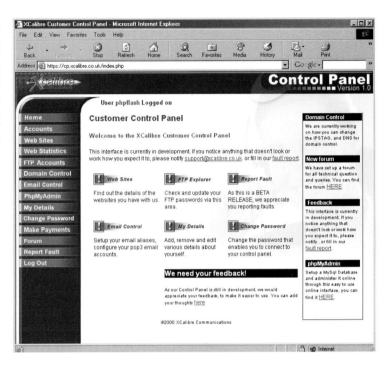

Sign up!

When you've made your final choices of domain and hosting package, sign up and complete the process. You will have chosen a username and password, and these will allow you access to your control panel functions.

> It usually takes 24-48 hours for your domain to be registered and configured, and available to view.

Uploading with Dreamweaver

Now that you have a site, or at least some plans on how to get one, we will look at uploading your website to the Internet. If you don't have your domain and website, you can follow along the instructions anyway, or come back to this section as the need arises.

We are going to be working in the Site window of Dreamweaver from now on.

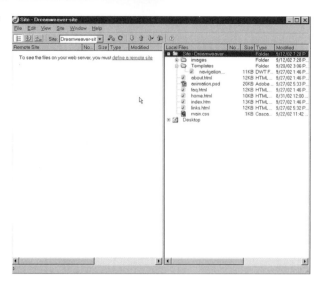

Connecting to the web server

We will now set up Dreamweaver to connect to our remote server (web hosting account):

1. Under Site, click on Edit Sites.

2. Choose the site to edit and click Edit again, or double-click the site name.

You will now see the Site Definition window again.

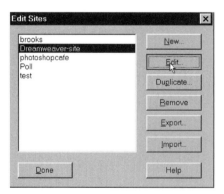

3. Click on the Advanced tab. You can use the Wizard (on the Basic tab) if you wish, but it's quicker to do it this way.

4. Choose Remote Info from the left-hand menu. This is where we will put all our hosting information.

5. Under Access choose **FTP**.

> *FTP or File Transfer Protocol is the most accepted way to upload files to the Internet. There are many third-party FTP programs, but with Dreamweaver's excellent built-in functions you really have no need for any external programs.*

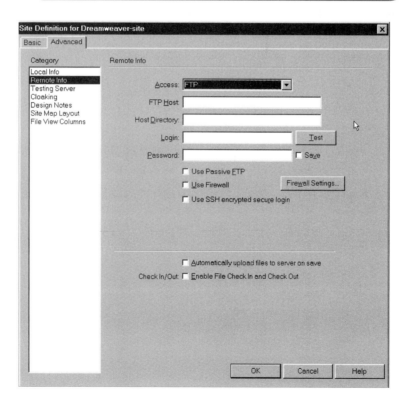

6. For FTP Host, enter the domain name for your website if it is operational.

7. Directory: This is the directory on the server where your files will be uploaded. Generally /www/ or /htdocs/ or /public_html/ are common. If you are not too sure, just leave this field blank or ask your web host.

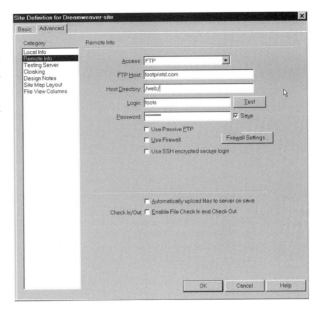

Your host's website may have tutorials outlining these details for new users.

8. Your Login and Password have been provided by your host (or chosen by you) when you signed up.

When you have entered all the information correctly, it's time to test the connection.

9. Press the Test button. This is a new feature in MX and is extremely useful!

10. If there is a problem with the information you entered or your computer is not connected to the Internet, you will see this message.

11. When everything is correct, this is the message that you will see. Click OK. Congratulations! We are now ready to move your website onto the Internet.

Uploading your files

Click the Connect button on the top of the Site window. When you are connected to the remote server you will see a green light on the button. Press the same button to disconnect.

All your local files will be located on the right pane and your remote server will be displayed in the left pane.

1. Select the files you wish to upload by clicking on them. Use the Cᴛʀʟ/Oᴘᴛɪᴏɴ key to select multiple files or click on the top and Sʜɪꜰᴛ+click on the bottom file to select them all.

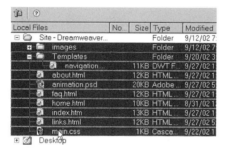

2. Press the Put button as shown or simply drag the files over to the other pane. This will put (or upload) all your selected files and folders to the remote computer. All the folders will be created on the remote server exactly as they are on your local computer, and this will mean all your links will work correctly.

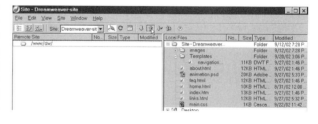

You will see a status bar to indicate that you are uploading files.

3. You will be asked if you want to include dependent files. Dependent files are all the images and assets that are associated with the HTML page(s) you are uploading. Click No because you are uploading all the files so the dependent files, will be uploaded anyway. This feature is useful if you are uploading a single HTML page and there are several new images associated with it.

When you have finished uploading you will see all your files and directories displayed in the remote pane. These files are now on your web hosting account and located on the web server.

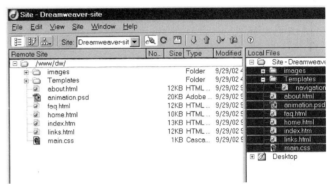

4. You can manage individual files on the remote server the same way you would locally. Select any file and right-click on it and you will see some options such as renaming and deleting. Let's delete the .psd file, since a web browser cannot display PSD formats anyway.

5. To download a file from the web server to your hard drive, select the file and click the Get button. This will overwrite your local copy of the file.

This may be useful if you have access to your site set up at work and at home, and have uploaded a more recent version from another location.

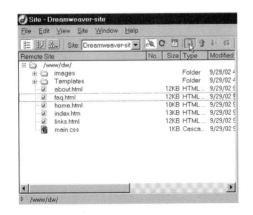

6.   If you wish to look at a log of all the activity on your FTP site, click the FTP Log button.

You will now see a display of all the activity on the FTP from Dreamweaver. This lets you track all the files you have been uploading and downloading and lets you spot any errors.

Matching content

Sometimes you will want to compare your local files with your remote files to make sure you have all the latest updates on your remote server.

To do this, connect to the server and select Site > Synchronize.

You will have the option of a single file, directory or the entire site to synchronize. You can also determine where the newest files will go. If the web server information is newer than the local computer, choose Newer from Remote. This is useful if other people have been working on the website and you want the latest updates, or you have been working on the site from a different computer.

The other option is Put newer files to remote. This is useful if you have been making a few changes and want to make sure they are all reflected on the website.

You could also compare the two and update the local and remote computers to both reflect the newest files. This is the option to choose when there have been changes to both the local and the remote files.

Click the Preview button. As a safeguard, Dreamweaver will not move any files yet, but will display a report and ask for authorization to transfer any files.

After Dreamweaver has examined both sites and compared the two, it will display a list of changed files. Uncheck the Action check box to have the file skipped, or check the box to have the file transferred.

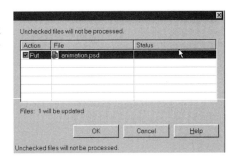

Here we skipped the PSD file that we deleted earlier on, we don't need to upload it to the server again. You might also want to move such files to a separate development folder.

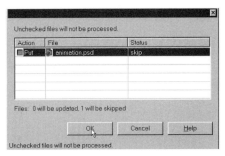

Finally you will see a message saying Synchronization complete. You now have the latest files uploaded to the web.

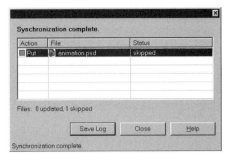

Lastly, open your browser, enter your URL and test your website.

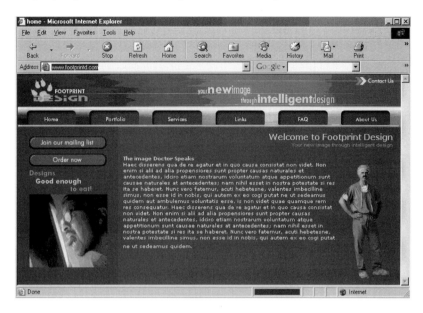

Summary

Congratulations, you have now built a website and served it on the web for the world to see! Don't forget to email the URL to all your friends and let them enjoy your handiwork. It's also useful to get some feedback from them to see how your page looks on different computers, browsers and operating systems. This final test may reveal a glitch or two that you have overlooked.

I encourage you to get as much experience as you can and build as many web pages that you can. You will just continue to get better and better. The very fact that you have invested the money and time to read this book tells me you are serious about building better than average pages, and you can do it!

Photoshop and Dreamweaver Pro Tips

In this section...

We'll run through a checklist of important tips for you to keep in mind when taking your site and your projects beyond the end of this book, touching in issues such as:

- Efficiently backing up your site and preparing for disaster recovery
- Working with your client
- Creating project-specific palettes and color schemes
- Some of Dreamweaver's neat workflow features
- Taking your skills further and keeping in touch with your peers

If all goes as planned, all of your sites from the first one on function perfectly and win every design award out there. Generally, though, nothing goes exactly as planned. No one likes to think of the things that can potentially go wrong with a site, but if there's anything that can be guaranteed, it's that something sometime will go wrong, therefore good planning and disaster recovery plans put in place from the inception of the site design are a great idea.

Disaster isn't inevitable. True, there are few people working in this industry who haven't experienced the heart-breaking frustration of a crashed hard drive or a major blunder. It's rare, however, that every single thing can go wrong at once, and the best thing is that many problems are avoidable or preventable with a few simple be-prepared steps.

The following checklist will help you streamline your workflow and ensure that you are prepared for any eventuality, bringing you some of the top tips for Photoshop, Dreamweaver, and web design in general to make your future site development, career, and work processes a little simpler.

1. Keep all original PSD files

It's a good practice to keep copies of all Photoshop PSD files, packed with all the layers of work that you poured your heart into, just in case of future changes or disasters.

It's crucial to hold on to all of your original files, not necessarily just PSDs. You might even want to keep them safe in a special development folder. If changes have to be made to graphics, to the layout, to names of areas on the site that you've made into slices or buttons, all you have to do is call up the original file and make the changes and save again.

When you make changes, give the file a new name, so that you have all significant versions of all PSDs. Tools that enforce version control like Microsoft Source Safe make this much easier. There are a number of open source and shareware version control programs that are also useful for this.

2. Keep a current back up of your site

Make sure you have at least two copies of everything in two different locations.

236

Always keep a backup of your site on removable media such as CD- or DVD-ROMs. If you have space you might also want to use a separate part of your hosting space to back up your PSDs, palettes and other work-in-progress or original files.

3. Keep backups of 'semi-final' sites

It's not just your final files that need good backing up!

While working with clients (and remember a client could just be your friend whose band needs a website done!), you'll probably make a number of prototypes to show them. Part of that process may have been working prototypes in Dreamweaver, in which you took sample content and art and created two to five sample sites from which the client then chose the final site design.

Keep these semi-final sites, just in case. Clients notoriously change their mind, and if you at least have a sample build of another design that they suddenly want, then you've saved a bit of time.

4. Keep a copy of files with client records

Burn a CD at the end of a project which contains all electronic documents relating to the project; e-mails, photos, site files and developers' notes, as well as any palettes etc. That way if you ever need to go back to the site at a later date, everything is together in one place for the next person to work on the project.

It's two years from now, you want to be able to access all pertinent information when an old client calls and asks if you can update their site. Pulling out files and doing a thorough browse through them (both paper ones and digital ones) will remind you of your previous experience with this client, the number of versions they requested, and files they may want to update and change with the times.

Even if the client wants a complete and total new look, reviewing these files – and impressing your client by having kept all of these files – will make the process easier. Proposing new designs with 'old' color swatches, digging out a PSD file from which the initial web logo was prepared so that it will be more easily changed; all of these smooth the process of creating a new look and feel.

5. Don't give clients access to areas they don't need

Unless you want your clients (especially the 'helpful' ones) to accidentally overwrite a file that you've spent a week working on, don't give your clients access to FTP sites, original files, or site servers.

If clients insist on having files or donating images, set up a standalone directory on your ftp site they can access.

6. Document your processes

Documenting processes are a way of keeping tabs on what is being done during the process, as well as tracking your process for future projects.

During the time you are working on your or a client's project, for example, at any point you or your client may wish to question why a certain decision was made, and how it was implemented. Why was this column added to a table, for example? What was the name of the file in which we save our custom palette? Who did what part of the process, and who did the other?

Also make sure you document anything unusual that happens, whether it seems like a software bug or maybe a problem with your computer. This will help you troubleshoot later.

You can use Dreamweaver's Design Notes under File > Design Notes... to make notes about each particular page.

7. Consider your update schedule

If you're promising a daily or weekly update to your site, are you prepared to do so? It's better to tell people "We're weekly now, but we'll be going daily in a few months!" than to promise daily updates and not deliver. Just as important is to make sure that if your site is used as a medium to give information about timely subjects, you maintain the site in a way that continues to portray your professional image. If you don't have the time or people power to do so, it may be a smarter move to delegate this aspect to others.

Making sure that the site is updateable by others authorized to do so, maybe even your client, is key. Make sure that anything people may have to adjust has well-placed comments that make sense.

Comments are useful for adding notes into the content of your pages, and they make it very easy to find your way around the HTML code of your pages. Insert a comment using the Comment button as pictured.

Above all, make sure your commitment to the ongoing project is realistic.

8. Create custom swatch palettes for projects

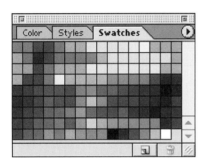

Creating custom swatches saves time down the line.

As mentioned in **Chapter 1**, you'll often find that a client may want to base their color scheme on company logo colors, a state or country flag colors, organizational uniform colors, holiday-specific color schemes, or just a select group of colors to build a site around.

It can be a tedious process, but if you've got to keep your or your client's artwork within a specific color palette and want to ensure that you stick to it (especially if you're creating a lot of site elements in Photoshop), you can customize swatches as you see fit. In the long run, this saves time (AKA money!). This will also save time later on if you do more work for the client based on the same palette. You can always add or subtract colors in future projects.

Any custom swatch palettes that you save show up in your Swatch menu the next time you restart Photoshop. Your custom swatch palettes are saved by default in Photoshop > Presets > Color Swatches, *and you need to save them here for them to appear on the menu. Find those that you've created for custom purposes and make copies for your client folders.*

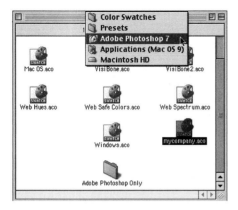

Creating custom swatches is also important if more than one person is working on graphics files for a client. One person makes the custom swatch, and then shares the swatch with everyone on the art/design team, and all color choices will be consistent.

And later, when the site is being considered for a redesign, some of its elements may be usable. For example, if you stick with the same color for backgrounds, using the same transparent buttons or images will not be a problem in the future, because the transparency and anti-aliasing colors should remain the same.

9. Play around with optimization

Take the time to play with files and get the best quality for file size as you can. If you're doing a lot of experimentation, be sure to start with the high-end file each time, so that you're not compressing an already compressed file.

Once you've found some settings that work well for the images of a certain kind on your site, save them. You can access these saved settings when working on other files, so that images have the same level of quality throughout.

10. Keep an eye on size

> *Even if you think that everyone in your audience has cable modems at home and T1 connections in their office, you should still try to keep file sizes down to a manageable size.*

While in general, people's connections keep getting faster, here's one area where you have to plan for the present, rather than the future, and design for what already exists. When you have proof that everyone in your market has a cable modem or faster, then file size may not matter as much.

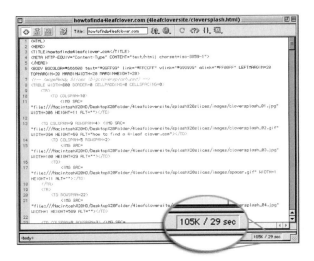

Even if your page is full of small images, those file sizes can add up fast. Dreamweaver can be set up to tell you what size your page is, as well as how many seconds the entire page will take to load on various connection speeds.

11. Clean up code

If you've been modifying any code in Dreamweaver, or imported pages that come from another editor or any other source, use Dreamweaver's Clean Up HTML command, under the Command menu.

Getting rid of excess tags assures that your page will work better and its overall size will be smaller. Reading code will be easier to comprehend, too. At this stage you're probably not going to be changing the code, but later in your Dreamweaver career it will probably become a necessity.

You'll notice the command beneath this one is Clean Up Word HTML. This is useful if you have exported documents or text from Microsoft Word as a web page and want to incorporate this without all the extra stuff Word likes to include.

12. Upload and test

While Dreamweaver is relatively smart in this area, it's crucial to take a test run through your site once you've uploaded files.

Even though Dreamweaver keeps track of where files are and where they should be, there could be an errant file that went off to a different directory and your page or image may not be showing up where you expect it to be once the site goes live. This is especially important if more than one person is working on the site.

You also want to get a feel for how the site feels and works out there in the real world: are images loading in the order you want them to? Is it taking forever for the entire page to show up?

13. Know how to use the Synchronize command

We covered this more fully in the last chapter, but I can't emphasize enough that you know exactly what you're accomplishing with the Dreamweaver Synchronize command.

In the wrong hands, this command can wipe out valuable files and work that you (or a co-worker) have invested a good amount of time in.

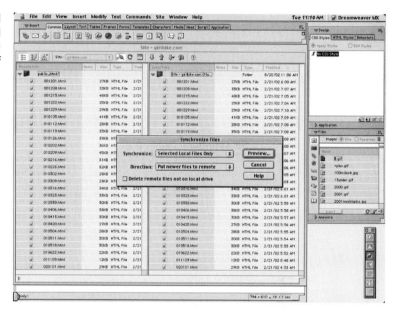

Know what you're going to synchronize before you just go ahead and click.

You might think that your local files are the newest ones, but what if a co-worker made changes earlier than you did, and uploaded those?

To see which files are newer, Windows users use Dreamweaver's Edit > Select Newer Local or Edit > Select Newer Remote, and Mac users choose Site > Site Files View > Select Newer Local or Site > Site Files View > Select Newer Remote.

In the Site panel, make sure that you have the site loaded that you want to synchronize and that you're connected to the server as well. You can synchronize specific files or folders, or the entire site.

14. Take advantage of automation

As we've already seen, templates and style sheets make things much easier for us, but Dreamweaver includes many more automation features.

As you learn about all the cool things in Dreamweaver hidden away in panel menus and sub-menus, you'll find tools that will make your work unbelievably easier.

Haven't you ever gone to a site and had a note come up that says something along the lines of "Hey, you don't have Netscape *n* or Flash Player version *n*, so we're redirecting you to the text/old version of our site," and then you're swept away to that alternate page? You can have Dreamweaver automatically include a similar script in your pages.

Dreamweaver comes with a number of automated behavior builders. We covered just the rollover behaviors but there are many more, mostly completely self-explanatory. Clicking on the Add Behavior [+] button brings up a menu with options. In this example, we're picking Check Plugin.

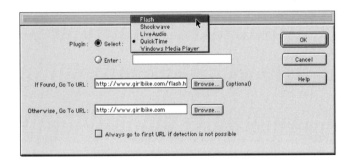

Dreamweaver can build a script that checks for Flash, Shockwave, LiveAudio, QuickTime, and Windows Media Player. You then specify which URL you want the user to go to if the plugin is found, and which URL you want them to go to if it isn't found (perhaps a less media-rich site or a page that lists links to download the Flash player or other software).

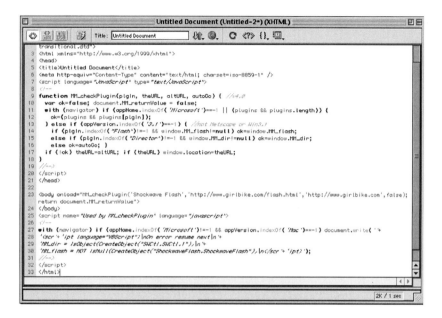

Voila! All the JavaScript necessary to perform this is generated automatically and is viewable by viewing code in your Dreamweaver document.

This kind of automated help is what gets work done more efficiently.

15. Join a user group or mailing list

> *Photoshop users are passionate about this image manipulating program in a way that you don't see many others in the web field, perhaps because of its long pre-web history in other media. Likewise, Dreamweaver also has a massive following. Now that you know something about both applications, take advantage of these communities.*

On newsgroups and lists you'll find answers to your questions, tips and just chat. Also, try Adobe Studio or Macromedia Exchange for more community-based support and information interchange from the manufacturers themselves.

Often user groups receive news from associated companies before the public or the press, are offered beta testing opportunities, and sometimes deals on software, discounts on event registration, and job listings.

16. Take it further

> Don't let the end of this book be the end of your journey. There's tons more to learn!

If you're like me, you have little spare time to spend taking full-on, in-depth, hands-on classes in web applications. But there's no way to keep ourselves marketable without knowing the ins and outs of applications, so it's a good idea to remain teachable and set aside time for lessons on your own time, if you can't get out of the house and go back to school full time.

These days, there are plenty of online and digital media classes you can take in a particular area of expertise, as well as software-specific courses that are targeted toward the web market. Books covering all aspects of using a specific application abound, and if you'll forgive a shameless plug, friends of ED have a great library of Photoshop and Dreamweaver books at www.friendsofed.com to expand and enhance your skills.

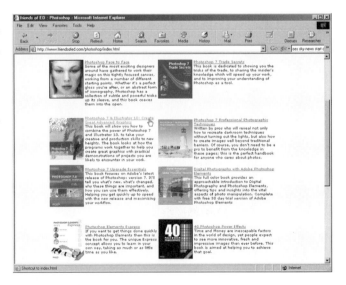

Other areas of web design and development, non-software specific areas that is, will serve to make your designing better, as well as your marketability. Attend a conference on usable web design, web marketing, e-commerce, or accessibility to supplement your software prowess with some more general industry awareness.

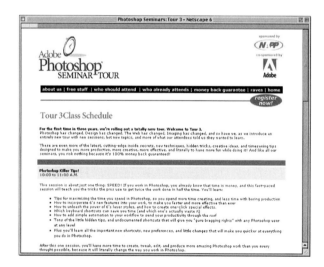

Both Macromedia and Adobe offer free and fee-paying events, application-wide (such as web development) and software-specific (such as Photoshop).

If you can get out for a few hours, and you live in an area close by to their locations, both Adobe and Macromedia go on tour to offer free classes on their products or paid conference events that generally have a more intensive focus, like Macromedia DevCon. Both also offer some online classes and tutorials – some free, some subscription-based.

17. Last but not least...

> *This may sound trite, but above all else, have fun, and take pride in your work!*

These are two programs that can do some amazing things, and we hope you'll have a lot of "a-ha!" moments as you plan, experiment, and create. Take on your projects with curiosity and enthusiasm, and keep an open mind to learning and discovering new techniques and practices.

Be patient with yourself and learn from your mistakes – both of these applications have a steep learning curve because they are chock-a-block full of really cool features.

Enjoy and get in touch with us to let us know about your achievements!

Index

The index is arranged hierarchically, in alphabetical order, with symbols preceding the letter A. Many second-level entries also occur as first-level entries. This is to ensure that you will find the information you require however you choose to search for it.

friends of ED particularly welcomes feedback on the layout and structure of this index. If you have any comments or criticisms, please contact: feedback@friendsofED.com

Macromedia Dreamweaver MX merges the faultless visual layout tools of Dreamweaver and the powerful yet easy-to-use database integration offered by UltraDev into a product that is simply the most vital piece of software any web designer can own.

Unlike many other books, Foundation Dreamweaver MX concentrates on both sides of this alliance, looking to the future. No matter what your background, this book will give you a solid foundation in graphic design and layout issues as well as a full grounding in the powerful database integration features that Dreamweaver MX offers.

The truth is that database integration is no more of an extra in today's climate than faultless visual design, and this book is here to guide you through this new world, covering dynamic scripting with PHP and the popular MySQL database.

This book is suitable for both PC and Mac (OS X needed) platforms.

Whether a complete novice or a past user, after reading this book, you'll be fluent in the full breadth of Dreamweaver MX's powerful functionality, a unique learning curve backed up by solid real-world case studies and tutorials.

What this book covers:

- Site design and layout principles
- Using templates and Cascading Style Sheets to create advanced site designs
- Adding interactivity to pages with script
- Setting up PHP and MySQL to create powerful dynamic database-driven applications

Dreamweaver MX makes this all possible, and Foundation Dreamweaver MX makes it easier than you could have imagined.

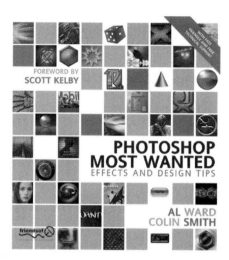

The best, most requested effects that you've seen on the Web and elsewhere, explained by two Photoshop Experts: Al Ward and Colin Smith. In response to feedback from their popular web sites and magazine articles, Al and Colin have teamed up with friends of ED to answer your questions. They've packed in lots of useful information, not just how to create a certain effect, but other tips too, like how to improve your workflow, variations on effects, and creative suggestions to help you express yourself further.

This book is for both the enthusiastic amateur and experienced pro alike - it's full of techniques and advice that will help Photoshop users from intermediate to advanced. This book will help you to stock up your armoury; you'll have a range of weapons for all occasions and be able to deploy them faster and more effectively.

The book is divided into three main sections; the first two are Al and Colin working individually to create the most wanted effects, and in the third section, Al and Colin combine their skills in three different design projects. These projects were selected to demonstrate how designers tackle a variety of tasks when working with others; the questions and issues that may arise, and how the final product is achieved.

The focus is on tutorials and how to create effects rather than lengthy descriptions of individual tools. The majority of requests that Al and Colin receive are about producing stunning images, not explaining the tools, so that's what they've concentrated on. We've kept one thing in mind during the making of this book: what do our readers really want?

Al and Colin found they didn't have the space or time on their sites (actionfx.com and PhotoshopCafe.com) to pass on all their knowledge to visitors - people kept asking them for more, more, more... so here it is: more information, more effects, more tips... and lots more!

Photoshop has helped to create an army of devoted followers, not by being relatively easy to pick up, but by having a huge range of creative options available to you once you have learned the basics. You can then let your imagination run wild...

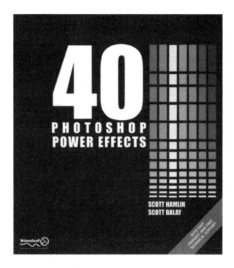

Whether you are new to Photoshop and want to produce some startling and impressive effects quickly, or you are a professional designer looking for inspiration and ground-breaking techniques to push your work to a new level, this book is for you. We've teamed up with top professionals from Eyeland Studio to show you how the experts do it.

Time and Money are inescapable factors in the world of design, yet people expect to see more innovative, fresh and impressive images than ever before. This book is aimed at helping you to achieve that goal.

In this book we aren't just trying to teach you new and innovative effects. The equally important objective of this book is to help you to get in the habit of using shortcuts and to utilize more streamlined techniques when working in Photoshop. The techniques in this book don't just show you how to create an interesting effect, they help you to get into the practice of using shortcut keys that trim precious seconds off the time it takes you to generate effects.

There is very little assumed knowledge of Photoshop, so even if you are a young designer at college, inexperiened in handling the digitial image, you will find the step-by-step tutorials clear, concise and easy to follow.

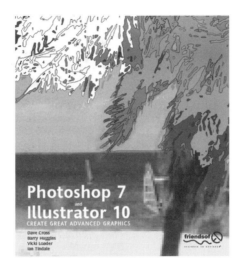

This book will show you how to combine the power of Photoshop 7 and Illustrator 10 to take your creative and production skills to new heights. Find out the best way to use them in tandem, with a seamless workflow, for stunning results in your print and web output. The book looks at how the programs work together to help you create great graphics with practical demonstrations of projects you are likely to encounter in your work.

You'll learn advanced techniques for working with layer blending modes, the latest tools and new file formats such as SVG, along with color management, animation, printing, web-publishing, and integration with other programs. This book is not for Photoshop and Illustator novices - it's called 'Advanced' because it aims to take your basic skills to the next level and teach you how to create the finest graphics you find in the world around you.

The book looks at how the programs can serve each other and you: Adobe has worked hard to make these two applications function more efficiently together - this book will help you to reap the rewards of their labor.

The aim of this book is to show how Photoshop 7 and illustrator 10 can work together as part of a team; this means looking at their strengths and weaknesses and how they compliment one another.

Part 1 is shorter than Part 2 and contains an analysis of each application; how each one performs certain tasks and where the crossover lies. Many functions can be acheived in both and there is a certain amount of personal choice involved - we evaluate the benefits of each one and which may be suited to certain tasks: we want you to find the right balance to maintain a long and happy marriage!

In Part 2, we look at the practical applications of each one through a series of projects that detail step-by-step how they may be used in conjunction with each other. The tutorials are backed up with theory and additional information to help you make an informed choice when deciding the workflow that fits you best. We hope to help you make the best use of your skills and talents, so you can go further and achieve more...

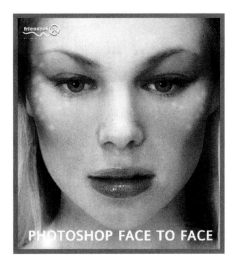

If we were to say Marilyn to you, what would you be thinking? Monroe? Manson?

Well, you would be thinking about the most inspired use of facial imagery. Anybody in advertizing will tell you the most effective sales tool around is the face. A face can sell you anything. Any product, any idea. And the most striking faces become icons in their own right.

With Adobe Photoshop, we can see the possibilities for facial stylization explode. This book looks at how to develop an image to get it right, and how to make these mugshots genuinely memorable.

Some of the most exciting designers around have gathered to work their magic on this tightly focused canvas, working from a number of different starting points. Whether it's a perfect gloss you're after, or an abstract form of iconography, Photoshop has a collection of subtle and powerful tricks up its sleeve, and this book coaxes them into the open.

This is a full color inspirations title, aimed at showing professionals and home users alike how to access the multiplicity of techniques available in Adobe Photoshop. By using such a familiar model as the human face, the effectiveness and originality of these techniques is thrown into sharp relief.

The book employs versions of Photoshop up to the brand new release Version 7, although the techniques shown will be compatible with previous releases of the software.

Each chapter contains multiple examples of how to treat a face in Photoshop, and an in-depth explanation of technique from the designer.

Notes

friendsof

D E S I G N E R   T O   D E S I G N E R ™

friends of ED writes books for you. Any suggestions, or ideas about how you want information given in your ideal book will be studied by our team. Your comments are always valued at friends of ED.

For technical support please contact support@friendsofed.com.

Free phone in USA:	800.873.9769
Fax:	312.893.8001
UK Telephone:	0121.258.8858
Fax:	0121.258.8868

Registration Code : 0578IAP4P588GQ01

From Photoshop to Dreamweaver: 3 steps to great visual web design– Registration Card

Name ....

Address ....

City ....State/Region ....

Country ....Postcode/Zip ....

E-mail ....

Profession: design student ☐ freelance designer ☐

part of an agency ☐ inhouse designer ☐

other (please specify) ....

Age: Under 20 ☐ 20-24 ☐ 25-29 ☐ 30-40 ☐ over 40 ☐

Do you use: mac ☐ pc ☐ both ☐

How did you hear about this book?..

☐ Book review (name)..

☐ Advertisement (name) ....

☐ Recommendation ....

☐ Catalog ....

☐ Other ....

Where did you buy this book? ....

☐ Bookstore (name) ....City...........................

☐ Computer Store (name)...

☐ Mail Order...

☐ Other...

How did you rate the overall content of this book?

Excellent ☐   Good ☐

Average ☐   Poor ☐

What applications/technologies do you intend to learn in the near future?...

....

What did you find most useful about this book? ....

....

What did you find the least useful about this book? ....

....

Please add any additional comments ....

....

What other subjects will you buy a computer book on soon?

....

What is the best computer book you have used this year?

....

Note: This information will only be used to keep you updated about new friends of ED titles and will not be used for any other purpose or passed to any other third party.

ISBN: 1903450578

friendsof

D E S I G N E R   T O   D E S I G N E R™

N.B. If you post the bounce back card below in the UK, please send it to:

friends of ED Ltd.,
30 Lincoln Road, Olton,
Birmingham, B27 6PA. UK.